HALFTIME

Marti Carelli-Gilbert

First Printing: July, 1990

Second Printing: September, 1990

Printed in the United States of America.

R.J. PRODUCTIONS
P.O. Box 210721
Nashville, TN 37221-0721

HALFTIME

by

Marti Carelli-Gilbert

For my sons,

Vincent and Ronald.

AUTHOR'S NOTE

The events in this book actually happened. Nothing has been changed, and the story has been recorded as accurately as memory allowed.

I want to thank Carol Shaughnessy, my editor, and my friends who gave me encouragement, patience and understanding when I needed them most.

PROLOGUE

November 20, 1970

"Good night, Vince. Mommy and Daddy love you," I whispered into my three-year-old son's ear as I gently released his tightened hold on me.

"Good night, Mommy, I love you," he answered, rolling over onto his tummy and snuggling beneath the covers.

Quietly, I walked over to three-month-old Ron's crib and peered over the top to make sure that all was well with him. He was sleeping peacefully on his stomach, with one arm stretched further above his head than the other.

Pulling an additional blanket over him, I turned and slowly went down the stairs into the kitchen. It was deserted. I picked up my writing paper and pen, and tiredly went over to the kitchen table. Every step I took seemed to be telling my utterly exhausted body to stop and rest.

Spent as I was, I knew that I had to write down what I could remember of the past six days, before it became a blurred memory. My in-laws were next door and this was my first opportunity to be alone. Wearily, I began to write.

Friday p.m.
November 20, 1970

My Dearest Vince,

Tonight I would like to take a little time to explain to you what happened on Saturday, November 14, 1970.

As usual, you and I were sitting on the couch watching television, while anxiously anticipating the return of your daddy from an out-of-state football game. We knew he would be depressed when he reached home, for his team had lost the game 20-17. Cheerfully, we bathed, put away the toys, and cuddled up together on the couch when...a bulletin flashed across the screen. It said that a DC-9 had gone down about one-half mile from the Huntington Tri-State Airport runway.

The next few moments were a void. I only know that, when I became aware again, I was crying and so were you. I wiped my eyes and told you all was well, but that I would be leaving to go see your Aunt Phyllis.

Dawn, your babysitter, came and Doris, our neighbor, took me frantically to Aunt Phyllis' house. Once there, we waited apprehensively for word of who was aboard that particular DC-9. We all knew that the Marshall University football team, coaching staff and numerous townspeople on board a DC-9 were overdue at the airport. Anxiously we waited...praying...crying...hoping against hope that our boys, husbands, and friends were not aboard the plane that had crashed. Then it came—positive identification—it was Marshall University's chartered DC-9.

Then we began to hope that there had been survivors. An hour later, we heard the radio announcer tearfully exclaim, "Tonight, at seven forty-seven p.m., a Southern Airlines DC-9 carrying the Marshall University football team, coaching staff, and some twenty townspeople crashed into the tops of some trees one-half mile short of the Huntington Tri-State Airport, flipped over, hit the side of the mountain, and then exploded...there were no survivors."

All hopes were dashed; the nightmare began. I returned home to find the house full of tearful people and you still up playing with your once put-away toys. I put you to bed and you asked no questions...then. The long hours of the night passed with friends. The next day you were sent to play with John-John and I went to comfort the other wives and friends who were involved.

That night, when you were getting ready for bed, you asked why Daddy had not come home. I said, "See the picture of Jesus above your bed? Daddy is with Him. Daddy will not be home again because Jesus now needs his help more than we do." You answered, "But I don't want Daddy to go away. I love him." I tried to explain it again. You went to bed—satisfied or not, I didn't know.

The next day began the long wait for notification that they had identified the body of your father. Late Tuesday evening, I received word that he had been identified, and that they would send me his wedding ring.

Wednesday, we flew to your grandparents' house to be with Daddy's mother and father.

Thursday night was the viewing, a time when friends look at the coffin and visit with the bereaved.

Your daddy's coffin was a beautiful mahogany with two brown-framed pictures of him on top. In the middle of the coffin was a large bouquet of flowers from me to your dad, and to the left was a large bouquet of flowers from you and Ron, addressed to "Dear Daddy." Flowers were all over the rooms. There were so many of them that the florists in South Jersey couldn't fill all the orders. Everything was beautiful and there were many people present who loved your daddy.

Friday morning, we went to the church, where there was a beautiful service in memory of your father. Friends carried him in his coffin from the church to the Gates of Heaven Cemetery where he was to be buried, and Father Kelly said prayers for him. Before I left, I put a white flower on top of his coffin, and a red rose on either side of it from you and your brother, Ron. His body is at rest, but his spirit is and always will be with you.

I will try to continue in you his enthusiasm and joy for life and keep in mind his memory always, although you were but three years old last Monday, November 16, 1970.

Love,
Mother

I dropped the pen onto the table, pushed my chair back and walked over to the refrigerator. For the first time in a week I was hungry. Writing all the details down on paper seemed to help my mind erase all the things I so desperately wanted to forget. Yet, it still didn't seem real. I felt that, at any moment, Al would walk through the door and I would find it had all been a ghastly nightmare. Pushing that unrealistic thought from my mind, I picked up my pen and began writing again.

Friday p.m.
November 20, 1970

My Dearest Ron,

You were barely three months old when your father was killed in a plane crash. I hope now that I can give you a few little insights into his wonderful character.

I'm going to take you back to the morning you were born. I had been under sedation and was not aware whether you were a girl or a boy. I will never forget your father's proud smile when he exclaimed, "It's a boy, Marti, a boy!" He was so very happy.

When we got home from the hospital, your daddy carried you into the house to show you to your brother, Vince. You were such a darling baby, and your father was very proud to have produced you.

Since you were born during football season, you never saw much of your father, nor he much of you. The times he was home he enjoyed cradling you in his arms. He would look down into your smiling face and say, "You don't know me, big fellow, but I love you very much."

The last night we all saw your father he made this statement to you—it was his last goodbye. "Come on, big fellow, give your daddy a little smile. You've changed so much I hardly recognize you. You don't know me now, but I'll make up for it later." He then kissed your small, beautiful cheek and left. That was the last time we ever saw your father.

Ron, he was a strong, kind, generous man who loved his sons above all, except God. He loved life, and in the short time he was here, he accomplished great things, mainly the deliverance of his sons to me. My only regret is that you'll never remember him—he loved you so very much.

Love,
Mother

As I finished the letters and neatly folded them into their envelopes, I felt at a loss. It would be years before Vince and Ron could understand what I had written to them about their father. There were so many things he had done that time would probably erase from my memory. Yet, as I wearily stood up from the table, gathered the letters together and headed toward my bedroom, I realized that there was a way to tell them after all. I would write Vince and Ron a story.

PART ONE

CHAPTER ONE

Spring, 1961

It was a beautiful day. The azure blue of the sky filled the bright spaces between the slightly swaying palm trees, making a pleasant contrast to the green softness of the grass. As I had done for the past month, I was excitedly awaiting the arrival of the postman. Today I just knew the letter would come, and I paced up and down the driveway, seashells crunching beneath my callused bare feet.

It seemed like ages since I had sent in my application to Lenoir Rhyne College, a small Lutheran school in Hickory, North Carolina. Dad, a Lutheran minister, was very pleased with my choice and I remembered him saying, "Well, Marti, now maybe you'll find some nice Lutheran guy to marry." He smiled, and I knew that he was proud to have his firstborn off to college. Since marriage was the last thing on my mind, I replied, "Don't worry, Dad, I want to go to college for other reasons, and I'm really anxious to see what North Carolina is like!"

As I waited, perspiration formed on my forehead. Even though it was early spring, the weather remained pleasantly around the low 70's—not bad for southwest Florida.

Then in the distance, I heard the muffled sound of a motorcycle coming my way. Nervously, I turned my head toward the sound and strained to see the road, which was lined with magnificent royal palm trees. As I watched, Mr. Duncan and his mail cart came into view. He slowly pulled up to our mailbox as I walked out to greet him.

"Hi, Marti! Let me see, it doesn't look like there's anything for you here today," he said with a twinkle in his eye.

"Come on, Mr. Duncan," I replied, frustrated. "Don't be a tease. Is it there or not?"

"Yes, it's here, and good luck," he answered, handing me a large, white envelope. I clasped the envelope to my chest while my heart pounded and anxious thoughts raced through my mind. What if I hadn't been accepted? What would I do then?

Slowly, I walked over to my favorite place in the yard, a palm tree with a curved trunk. I had often spent hours beneath this tree, with my back fitted comfortably into its natural curve. It had been my reading haven, where I found relaxation in delving into hundreds of historical novels.

But now, this moment before opening the letter of acceptance or rejection, it seemed alien. Before I realized what I had done, the letter was open and I was greedily reading.

"Dear Martha Bergstresser...We are happy to inform you that you have been accepted..."

That was all I was able to read, for I was running happily toward the house to tell my family the good news.

Thus began the first path which was to lead down an ever-winding trail of apprehension, turmoil, stability, desire, affection, love, happiness, elation, bewilderment, desolation and finally acceptance.

CHAPTER TWO

September, 1961

The odors of gasoline and perspiration were strong in my nostrils. It was a humid September day and the sounds of laughter, crying babies and snoring had no effect on my growing excitement. The Trailways bus was only minutes from my destination—Hickory, North Carolina. The twenty-four-hour ride had seemingly flashed by as I peered from my window at the gracious rolling mountains.

As the bus pulled into the rundown station, apprehension caught at me. Here I was in a strange city, and suddenly I realized that I knew no one.

With the help of a cabdriver, I was soon on my way to the campus. I had never seen it before, but I was praying it would be as lovely as several other campuses I had passed on my way.

As the Yellow Cab rolled up to the Administration Building, my hopes were fulfilled, for the sight that confronted me was magnificent. The Administration Building was a Gothic structure, and looked odd amidst the numerous modern "space age" buildings surrounding it.

My attention was caught by the tall pine and oak trees which populated the main campus area. Beneath them were stone benches occupied by several students holding hands. Everyone seemed so carefree. My tensions vanished as an upperclassman came over to help me.

Soon registration was completed and it was time to get settled in my new home for the next nine months, Fritz Hall. When I arrived there, I was unprepared for the reception awaiting me.

Several freshman girls were in front of me and as they approached the entrance they were surrounded by twenty or thirty boys. Boys, however, is not an accurate term—they looked more like a herd of bull moose, since hardly one of them was under six feet or two hundred pounds! Knowing that only freshmen were supposed to be there, I was puzzled by the appearance of this new breed. It could mean only one thing—that Highland Hall was the dormitory next to Fritz Hall. Anyone who knew anything knew that Highland housed most of Lenoir Rhyne's championship football team.

With renewed interest, I listened to the taunts of the boys and the giggles of the girls. I watched as the girls, made bold by each other's company, darted safely past the boys into the dormitory.

Knowing it was my turn next, I clutched my pillow for support. My pillow! With mounting horror, I realized I still held the pillow I had used on the long bus ride. I tried to collect myself, but it was already too late. The boys were making a complete circle around me, for they had no intention of letting an opportunity like this pass them by. As the first boy spoke, my mind was busily working out a solution to this strange predicament.

"Well, Pete, look what we have here. A wench who's advertising," the unknown blond said with a smirk as he caressed the pillow I held in my left hand. The boy addressed as Pete sauntered toward me and asked, "Where in this vast United States do you come from?"

"Fort Myers, Florida," I meekly replied, my dignity slightly ruffled by the big blond's opening comment.

"Well, I'll be a speckled pup!" Pete shouted as he bodily picked me up and twirled me around. "That's home to me, too. I'm from Venice; just a hop, skip and jump from little ol' Fort Myers." And with that statement, he gently lowered me to the ground.

Another boy, this one with thinning black hair, chimed in with a slang expression I had never heard before.

"Do they make out in Florida, too, ah...what's your name?" he asked.

"Marti," I answered, thinking what to say to that one. I wanted to come out with some clever stinging remark, but, as usual, nothing terrific hit me.

"What is 'make out'?" I asked, even though I had a fairly good idea. With that naive question, the place was in an uproar and I was becoming more embarrassed than ever. However, the boys' next question was a perfect lead-in to my premeditated plan.

"Come on, Marti, don't put us on. Whaddaya mean, you never heard of 'make out' before?"

"You don't understand. It's not that I've been out of communication with today's world, but for the past fourteen years I've lived on the Seminole Indian reservation," I answered innocently, and continued before anyone could interrupt. "I'm the adopted daughter of Osceola, the Seminole Indian chief. When I was three, my father was killed in the Everglades by a water moccasin and that left me alone, since my mother had died when I was born. The Indians took care of me and are now sending me to college."

When I finished this narrative, it was quiet enough to hear the boys' breathing. Immediately, their mood changed, and before I knew what was happening, they had taken over and were escorting me to my room.

I chuckled inwardly at this newfound attention and wondered at the unexpected response. At least, for the time being, I had turned the embarrassment away from myself, and would enjoy the boys' protectiveness for some months to come. At the moment, the deception was immaterial, and I felt as if I had stepped over one of the many hurdles to come.

Following tradition, during my first year my interests were centered around the upperclassmen. Thus, I was unaware of the watchful eyes of one freshman rookie...Al Carelli.

For the first year and the next, I found myself traveling the narrow pathways of apprehension and turmoil so normal to college students. Emerging, at last, in the middle of my junior year, I stumbled onto stability where desire lurked around an unseen corner.

CHAPTER THREE

February, 1964

As I sat at the cluttered desk in my dorm room, I could hear icy winds whistling outside my darkened windowpanes. February in North Carolina was one of the dreariest months of the year, and it always seemed to have a similar effect on my moods. Restlessly, I threw down my pen and abandoned any notions of continuing my homework.

Turning in my chair, I saw Betty, my roommate, emerge from the bathtub. She was busily preparing for her date with Ronnie, her latest beau. It was a wonder that Betty and I ever got along, for our personalities were always in opposition and our backgrounds were entirely different.

Betty, delicate in build, was from a wealthy southern family and never had to concern herself with anything but her activities and studies. She had grown up knowing what was properly accepted in southern society; while I, born of northern parents who were dedicated to their religious beliefs, had lived a modest life in Florida. My parents didn't have the financial ability to send me to college, so I had been working at school and during the summers to earn the necessary money to complete my education. To Betty I seemed rather outspoken, which stemmed from my straightforward upbringing.

Yet now it was Betty who asked a blunt question. "What's with you, Marti? You act like you're so nervous. Are the preparations for the wedding finally getting to you?"

"Who knows?" I responded with a shrug, and she hurriedly left the room. The wedding! What an undertaking that was going to be. Pat and I had dated all my freshman and sophomore years, and then he had gone on to graduate school in New York. This past Christmas when we visited my family, it seemed only natural that we should get engaged. The wedding was to take place this

June, one year before I was to graduate. But it had been two months since I had seen Pat, and I was getting restless.

Once again, I returned to my homework, but to no avail. Pushing the chair back, I got to my feet, grabbed a jacket and headed out of the dorm toward the Bear's Den. Surely there would be something going on there! Anything was better than just sitting and doing nothing.

As I approached the Student Union building I could hear the music and laughter within. It sounded pretty rowdy for a weeknight and I guessed there were quite a few others who were also restless. As I entered the Bear's Den, a dance area with a jukebox and decorated with the pennants of rival schools, I noticed several couples dancing, playing cards, and just talking. Since Lenoir Rhyne was a small school, everyone knew each other and I didn't feel awkward as I sauntered over to the nearest group of girls and boys seated around a card table.

"What's up?" I inquired.

"Nothing much," answered Lefty, one of our more coordinated basketball players.

It wasn't long before I was dancing with several different boys and beginning to come out of my restless mood. Soon there was a large group gathered around and one of the boys made a suggestion.

"Why don't we all go to the Green Valley for a beer? How many cars do we have among us?" he asked.

"I have enough money for four beers, and I've got a car too," answered Hyski, one of the football players present.

"Good enough," I said, and followed after Hyski while Doris and Geach, another couple, were close behind.

I knew Hyski as well as I knew most of the other people present. He was in my class and ran with the same crowd I did, although we had never dated. As we entered the car, Geach made a suggestion.

"Why don't we go to my house in Statesville? My parents are in Europe and the Beatles will be on television tonight and we can watch the color set." It seemed like a great idea, since there were no color sets on campus and everyone was dying to see how the Beatles performed—they were the newest rage.

We covered the twenty miles between Hickory and Statesville in no time and pulled up before a beautiful brick home. As we got out of the car Hyski had borrowed from a friend, Geach opened the front door and led us into a small den filled with family portraits.

After turning on the television, Geach and Doris disappeared. I didn't miss them, however, because as I crossed the room to find a chair, Hyski pulled me down onto his lap. At once I felt uncomfortable. For some reason, I was always getting myself into predicaments like that, and I tried desperately to think of some way to make Hyski understand that I really <u>had</u> come along for the pleasure of being in someone's company and to watch the Beatles perform. Nonchalantly, he pulled me toward him and as I pulled away, the kiss intended for my lips grazed the top of my head.

"Hyski, you know I'm engaged to Pat, and I honestly didn't come along for a lovemaking session," I tried to explain.

"Look, Marti, I haven't had a date in two weeks. How do you think I feel?" He pulled me to him again.

I didn't know whether to laugh or cry. It had been over two months since I had even been held, let alone kissed, and his attitude irritated me. While I tried to think of some reply, I noticed how handsome he really was. He had quite a muscular body within his six-foot frame, and I noticed several scars on his arms, which he had probably received playing football. His dark hair and deep brown eyes went rather well with his large nose and square jaw. His olive skin only seemed to set off his Italian features. In that one glance, I could see how Hyski probably got his way with most women. This time he had come up against more than he had bargained for, and I decided that conversation was what was lacking.

"You know, Hyski, I've known you all these years but I don't even know what your real first name is," I said.

"Hyski was a nickname given to me by friends because I always talked about a disc jockey back home who called himself Hyski-O-Rooti-McVadi-O-Zoot. No one could remember the entire name so Hyski stuck. My first name is Al, Al Carelli," he replied.

The rest of the evening was spent in conversation about our families and funny things that had happened to each of us in the years before college. We really enjoyed the Beatles' concert, and just before we were ready to leave, Hyski looked at me and said, "You know, Marti, you're something else." And this time when he pulled me to him, I didn't argue and felt a stirring within me from his kiss that should not have been there.

On the way home, the car radio played one of the Beatles' songs, *I Want to Hold Your Hand*, and Hyski, with a wink and smile, held my hand in his.

I checked in and returned to my room. Before I had even taken off my jacket, Betty inquired, "What's this I hear about you and Hyski taking off for the evening?"

"Oh, it was nothing. Just a fun night together," I replied, but went immediately to my desk to write a letter to Pat. I didn't think anything would ever develop between Hyski and me, but I had learned one thing from the evening's encounter. I was not ready to get married yet and couldn't keep that secret from Pat.

After that, Hyski and I dated several times, and on campus became known as the newest couple, but it was the end of March before he asked to take me to the Presentation Ball. This was an occasion when the new pledges and sisters were formally presented to the fraternities and sororities, and each year it seemed to grow into a more glamorous affair. We would be double-dating with my suite-mate, Barbara, and her date.

The night finally arrived and I was anxious to make a new impression on Hyski. Up until that time, he had only seen me in my usual sporty clothes and probably never believed I could actually walk in heels, let alone in a formal gown. As Barbara finished dressing, I gallantly practiced my entrance.

"Gee, Barbara, you'll have to walk ahead of me into the room. It would look ridiculous for us to walk together. Even with you in heels there's too much of a contrast in height," I said.

Barbara was barely five feet tall and I was a good eight inches taller. Nervously we walked down the stairs together, and as pre-planned, she entered first. All my tiring preparations were worth the startled expression on Hyski's face when he first saw me. Together we left for the dance.

The evening was full of excitement. I don't know quite when it happened, but sometime during the night I realized that my affection for Hyski went far deeper than I had imagined. When we returned to the dorm and were saying good night, we looked into each other's eyes and knew we were both feeling the same desire. As he held me close, he whispered into my ear, "I love you, Marti." And I answered, "I also love you, Hyski."

Not too many weeks later, our junior year was just about to end and preparations for summer jobs were underway. I was reading over a letter to my parents, explaining that I was taking the summer to work up and down the east coast with a girlfriend, when Hyski came running up to me with the largest smile on his face I had ever seen.

"Marti, guess what? I got it!" he said, his eyes shining.

"Got what, Hyski?"

"The boys voted me next year's captain of the football team," he said breathlessly. "I'm so excited and anxious to get started. I just know I can do a good job for them!"

I felt warm and happy inside to see his pleasure. This meant the upcoming school year would be sort of like every girl's dream, for I would be chief cheerleader and he would be captain of the football team. We would get to attend all the football games together, and in a sense, would be participating in the same sport. Everything pointed to a successful senior year.

Then the term ended and Hyski and I said our goodbyes, promising to write during the summer. We were both eagerly looking forward to the coming of fall.

CHAPTER FOUR

August, 1964

As I shivered, I pulled the covers tightly around my head. The bells had rung, but there would be a few moments of peace before all hell broke loose. Without peering from beneath the warmth of my blankets, I knew it would be another cold, rainy Maine day. Gathering courage, I threw the bedcovers back and vigorously jumped out of bed. The instant my bare feet touched the hard, uncovered floor, chills swept through my body. With teeth chattering, I began my first duties of the day.

"Okay! Everybody up and out! You've got just fifteen minutes until flag raising. Sherry, Barbara, Linda, Scotti—MOVE IT!" I shouted as everyone slowly began to move, emitting moans and groans. Glancing at my watch, I noticed that it was already after six a.m., so we would be late again—par for the course!

"Don't forget to put on your raincoats and boots," I reminded everyone as I peered out the window toward Brenda's cabin. Everything seemed to be going smoothly over there.

I laughed to myself as I recalled how Brenda and I, physical education majors together at Lenoir Rhyne, had started out working in Myrtle Beach, South Carolina as waitresses, but had ended up working as counselors at Camp Mataponi in Naples, Maine.

****

For me, the summer was to be free from financial worries, for with a government loan and my savings, I had enough money to get through my senior year. With relief I had quit the waterfront director's job I had held for three years at Camp Emanuel in Groveland, Florida. It had become too nerve-racking for me—every summer I had lived in dread that someone would drown in the murky waters of the lake. When Brenda had suggested we find jobs at Myrtle Beach, I was all for it.

We were there for three weeks when Brenda received a call from a resort in Naples, Maine, saying she was needed as a waitress there. Brenda wouldn't leave without me, so off we went.

That little adventure lasted one week. Soon after arriving, we realized there were too many waitresses for us to make the kind of money we wanted, so I began looking around for another suitable job. Luckily, I walked into Camp Mataponi the morning before the campers were to arrive, and found they were in need of another swimming instructor. It was very unorthodox for them to hire people on the spot, and they weren't so sure that we wouldn't be leaving as we had done twice already. Nevertheless, they hired "the vagabonds from North Carolina".

Our working conditions were quite pleasant. Mataponi reminded me more of a country club than a camp. The only real inconvenience was the lack of heat and showers in the cabins. Because the camp was situated in the mountains along the side of East Sebago Lake, it was prey to low summer temperatures. For this reason, the girls rarely saw me without sweaters or sweatshirts. Even while teaching swimming, I strolled up and down the dock bundled in warm-ups.

****

A brisk knock at the door brought me back to the present. Hastily, I looked at my watch...six twenty-five! We would surely have clean-up duties today.

"They sent me to fetch ya'll," Brenda shouted as the girls giggled at her southern drawl.

"We're on our way," I answered, hurriedly lining the girls up in front of the door and leading them outside.

Hours later, the bell rang, signifying that the last class of the morning was over. The girls scurried out of the water, grasped their towels and ran for their cabins to change.

"Hungry, Marti?" asked Skip, the waterskiing instructor, with a chuckle. It was no secret that I ate as if every meal were my last.

"You bet!" I answered, gathering up my teaching materials and heading toward the dining hall. As I passed the mail station, I wondered if there would be a letter from Hyski. He certainly wasn't much of a writer—it was the middle of August, with just two weeks of camp left, and I had received only three letters from him.

As I entered the dining hall and approached my seat, I saw that the mailman had left several letters next to my plate, as was the camp custom. Glancing through them quickly after I sat down, I realized none of them were from Hyski. Slowly, I opened a letter from Nancy, a sorority sister of mine. I began reading.

"I thought you might like to know that Hyski has been dating a cute transfer student from Georgia most of the second session of summer school," she wrote.

"Why does everyone assume that people like to hear about things like this?" I said to Brenda as she sat down beside me.

"Hear about what?" she inquired, and began reading the letter I handed to her. A sickening sensation was surging through my body.

"You haven't exactly been a saint yourself," said Brenda as she finished the letter. She put her napkin in her lap and began to eat.

"I realize Hyski and I have made no commitments, and it's not his dating that bothers me. It's just hearing about it—or at least I think it is," I answered soberly.

"Are you going to let some girl who won't even be there next semester bother you?"

"No, I'm not! In fact, a little competition is good for the ego, provided you win," I said and began eating my vegetable soup. "I'll know soon enough how Hyski feels about me with only one month left before classes begin." With that statement, I greedily consumed the remainder of my lunch.

CHAPTER FIVE

September, 1964

"Oh, mighty senior, I shall bow down before you and kiss your feet, if you so wish it," solemnly stated a skinny freshman boy as he awkwardly began to bend at the waist.

"No, Rat, that won't be necessary, but please take these papers over to the Student Union and give them to the secretary in charge," I answered with a laugh.

The freshmen had arrived yesterday for their week of orientation, and the Campus Guides were preparing them for the trials of Rat Week, which would officially begin with the arrival of the upperclassmen.

Serving as a Campus Guide was fun, and enabled me to get settled a week before everyone else arrived. The football players had been on campus for about a week, and even though I had been back almost three days, I still hadn't run into Hyski. When I completed my duties for the day, I decided to run over to the football field to watch practice.

As I passed through the gates, I took off my sweater and tied it around my shoulders. Looking up, I noticed that the boys were still doing individual drills. When the whistles blew, everyone ran to the center of the field and automatically divided up into two separate teams for scrimmage. I scanned the players for Hyski, but without their numbered jerseys, it was hard to tell one player from another. I looked to the line and found the center. I realized it was Hyski as he snapped the ball to Tom, the tailback.

The play gained about ten yards and everyone cheered. The spirit seemed to be high, considering the treacherous North Carolina heat. As Hyski raised his hand, the team gathered into the huddle, and I noticed him praise the boy who had run the ten yards. The next play was a completed pass to the end zone for a touchdown. Then the other team got the ball and Hyski remained in the game on defense. The first and second plays ended at the line of scrimmage. The third play was the expected pass, and the ball bounced off Hyski's outstretched hand.

****

At once, my mind went back to our freshman year, when Hyski intercepted a pass while playing East Carolina on their home territory. It was odd that I should remember that play for at the time I only had eyes for Pat, a tackle. I remember how surprised Hyski was when he realized he actually retained possession of the ball. After a few seconds of stumbling around, he ran with all his might toward the goal line. Every stride gave evidence that his powerful body was not as quick as his pursuers, and several yards from the goal line, he went down amidst the flailing arms and legs of the opposition.

Undaunted, he sprang to his feet and hastily returned to the bench, his hand held high with his fingers making a "V" for victory. What caught my eye as he passed me was his broad grin, exposing his missing front teeth, which had been knocked out in the game! It was the only time I ever saw Hyski smile openly on the field.

****

When I forced my mind back to the present, the boys had finished for the day and were slowly heading toward the field house. I noticed Hyski walking with several other players, and decided this wasn't the time for our first meeting, so I slipped unnoticed out of the side gate.

Later that evening, I was heading toward my dormitory after stopping at the snack bar for an ice cream cone when I ran into Hyski and a few of his friends.

"Marti! I didn't know you were here already!" Hyski exclaimed, rather startled.

"I've been here for a few days. It's good to see you. How have you been?" I asked, trying to cover my embarrassment at this unforeseen meeting.

"Gee, Marti, I'd like to see you tonight, but I've already made plans. Besides, tomorrow is a practice day and I'd have to be in early. How about tomorrow night? It's Saturday and we don't have to be in until midnight. Is it a date?" he asked nonchalantly.

"It's a date," I said. "See you tomorrow." With that, I went back to the dorm rather disillusioned. It certainly hadn't been the romantic first meeting I had pictured.

The next night, I was getting ready for our date when a voice over the intercom announced that I had a visitor in the lounge. I glanced at the clock. It was just seven, and Hyski was earlier than he had ever been. Puzzled, I went over to the box on the wall, pushed the button and answered, "I'll be down in about ten minutes. Will you please tell Hyski I'll hurry?"

"Yes," came the unfamiliar voice. This was a switch. Usually I was ready long before Hyski ever called. Dashing around my room, I put away my makeup, slipped a blouse over my head, stepped into my newest kilt outfit, pulled on my knee socks, found my loafers, paused before the mirror and hastened out the door.

When I opened the door to the lounge, I noticed how Hyski's muscular body seemed to fill the entire room. He was dressed comfortably in slacks and a short-sleeved shirt.

"Those short kilts sure do something for a girl's figure," Hyski said as his eyes wandered over me.

"You look mighty nice yourself," I replied, realizing how much I had looked forward to seeing him again.

"Why don't we just take a walk around the campus tonight? It's a warm evening and rather quiet since not many kids have arrived yet." When I agreed, he took my hand and led me out onto the porch.

It was an elegant evening, with the moon gleaming between the branches of the trees. As we strolled slowly over the campus, our conversation centered around what each of us had done during the summer months. Eventually, we ended up at the football stadium.

"Doesn't the field look good since they enlarged it?" Hyski asked.

"Yes, it does, and I'm getting butterflies just thinking about the start of the season," I answered.

"Me too, but I know the boys can have a successful season if they just put their minds to it. We don't have the depth that we had last year, or the experience, but, damn, I know we can do it!"

Then Hyski turned to me and said, "Marti, I brought you here for a very special reason. I can't tell you how much I missed you this summer, and I really wanted to be with you last night. I didn't want to go out anywhere special tonight because I wanted to see if I still had the same feeling I had for you last spring. Now I know I do." He paused and pulled something out of his pocket. "Will you take my fraternity pin and wear it so everyone will know how we feel about each other?"

I was so startled that I didn't answer immediately. This was the last thing I had expected, and I felt my heart pounding so hard that I thought it would burst. I realized my hesitation was worrying him, so gathering my thoughts, I answered, "Hyski, I never dreamed you'd ask me that tonight, and I can only say that I would be very proud to wear it."

Then he somewhat clumsily fastened his TKE pin to the left side of my blouse. Holding me close, he huskily whispered into my ear, "I've never felt this way about any girl before. My summer was so lonely without you, and all I know is that I want you with me now."

My thoughts went back to my summer and I realized that even while I was dating, I had been frustrated and restless, never understanding the cause of my discontent. In this one evening it all became so clear. All along I had had a deeper feeling for Hyski than I had wanted to admit. Maybe it was a protective shield I had raised to prevent myself from being hurt. Whatever, Hyski made me realize if you truly felt something for someone, then time, distance and lack of communication didn't interfere with that feeling.

"Hyski, you've made me wonderfully happy! This is a wonderful way to start out our senior year together," I replied as he bent down to kiss me.

"I know what we'll do!" he said suddenly. "Let's go over to the music building. I want to play the piano."

In all the years I'd known him, I'd never heard of Hyski playing the piano. Immediately I was suspicious.

"What's on your mind? Are you planning to get me into one of those soundproof rooms so that no one will hear my shouts of protest?" I asked jokingly.

"No, I really want to play the piano."

Even though I didn't believe for one minute that that was what he intended to do in the music building, I followed him. We entered the dimly-lit building, climbed the stairs and found a deserted room with a piano. Before turning on the lights, he passionately pulled me toward him.

"Wait a minute!" I protested. "I want to hear you play something." I waited to hear him confess to his real reason for coming here. But, to my astonishment, he went over to the piano, placed his fingers on the keys, and magnificently played *Take Five*.

CHAPTER SIX

October, 1964

"Calm down, it won't be all that bad," Hyski reassured me as we drove up to the entrance of a local motel.

"Are you positive I look all right?" I nervously smoothed down my medium-length hair for the tenth time.

"Damn it! It's not as if you were going to meet the President of the United States! It's only my mother, father, sister, and uncle, and I'm sure they'll love you at first sight," he impatiently answered.

Hyski's parents, who had never seen him play college ball, had come down for Homecoming weekend—but I wasn't so sure about this love at first sight bit. Hyski was the only son of two only children, and had been brought up in a strict Catholic home. It was no secret to his parents that I was a Lutheran minister's daughter, and I was positive they'd be looking me over to see what seemed to attract their son.

"People from New Jersey aren't that bad. Trust me. I know my folks—they'll take right to you," he reassured me again as he opened his car door. While he came around to open my door, I took one last glance in the rearview mirror, and tried unsuccessfully to calm my nervous stomach.

As gracefully as possible, I slid out of the seat, took Hyski's hand and proceeded toward the motel restaurant.

When we walked in, I spotted four people sitting in a booth near the side door of the restaurant, and knew at once they were Hyski's relatives. As we approached the booth, the attractive middle-aged woman and young girl sprang to their feet and embraced Hyski, while the men shook his hand.

"Mom, Dad, Uncle Howard, Linda, I'd like you to meet Marti," Hyski said as he gently pulled me forward. Surveying the group, I replied, "I've heard so much about ya'll that it's a pleasure to finally meet you."

"I must admit, we've heard a lot about you too, Marti," said Mrs. Carelli. "Won't you sit down so we can order something to eat? I'm starving!"

At once, my apprehension disappeared and we were talking together as if we'd known each other for years. While Hyski talked, I studied the group. To my astonishment, I realized how much he looked like his father. If I hadn't known better, I would have thought Hyski's father was his older brother. The only big difference between the two was height—Mr. Carelli was a large man, but about four inches shorter than his son.

"We have tickets for the concert tomorrow night featuring the Lettermen," Hyski announced. "I hope you'll enjoy it."

"That's great!" answered Linda. She had been extremely quiet up to that point, and her comment opened a way for some discussion.

"Would you like to spend tomorrow night in the dorm with me, Linda? It might be interesting for you to get a look at college life. Won't you finish high school soon?" I inquired.

"I have a few more years to go, but sure, I'd love to."

"Maybe you'd even like to help us decorate the car the cheerleaders will be using in the Homecoming parade," I suggested.

By the time dinner was finished, we'd made our plans for the following day. The Carellis would pick me up for dinner while Hyski ate with the team. We would all meet at Hyski's dormitory and go from there to the concert. Goodbyes said, Hyski and I returned to the campus.

"I really enjoyed the evening. It was senseless to have been so nervous," I told him. "Your parents couldn't have made me feel more at home."

"I'm happy you liked them. They're good people and I really wanted you all to get along. Well, I'd better hurry back to my room before bed check. We've got a big day ahead of us," Hyski said as he kissed me goodnight and left.

As I checked back in to my dorm, I heard my name called over the intercom system, and went to see what the trouble was.

"I'm right here, Nancy," I said to my short, chubby roommate. She had drawn hostess duty for the weekend, a fate no one enjoyed.

"It's the telephone. A call on line 42," she answered.

"Give me a minute to run upstairs. I'll take it up there." I ran down the hallway and took the steps two at a time.

"Hello," I answered. "This is Marti speaking."

"Marti, this is Susan. I thought you'd want to know that Pat's younger brother died today. His family will be seeing friends at their home tomorrow."

The news hit me hard, but I tried to pull myself together. "I'm surprised it happened so fast, Susan. I only heard he had cancer a few months ago. Thanks for calling. I really appreciate it," I said and slowly hung up the telephone. I felt sick inside. Except for my last meeting with Craig, Pat's eighteen-year-old brother, I remembered him as a vivacious teenager.

Even though Pat and I had broken off our relationship, we had seen each other briefly before the start of the year, and he informed me that Craig had been sent home from the Navy with cancer, and had been given only a short time to live. When I visited Craig later, he had looked very different, but his spirits had been high.

He was completely aware of the fact that he would soon die, but now that the expected had happened, it all seemed so unreal to me. Death seemed to be the one thing that no one actually believed would happen, yet was inevitable. Confused thoughts went through my mind. I wondered how God could allow an eighteen-year-old boy to suffer as Craig had done. All of a sudden, the things my father preached from his pulpit didn't make much sense to me. I returned to my room and had just lain down when Nancy came through the door.

"Going to bed already?" asked Nancy, a virtual night owl.

"No, I'm just thinking. Susan called tonight and told me Pat's brother died today," I answered.

"I'm sorry, Marti. What can you say when something like that happens?"

"You know, Nancy, life doesn't make much sense to me. I just can't seem to get my thoughts straight. How come some people live to be eighty years old and never do anything but steal, murder, and cheat? Craig was a good Christian boy who led a good life but only lived to be eighteen," I said, my voice rising.

"You know what they say, 'The good die young'," commented Nancy with a shrug.

"Not good enough! Jesus taught that the meek shall inherit the kingdom of heaven, but who knows what or where that is? When I ask my father questions like that, he tells me I just have to have faith in God. Good grief! It seems to me all that ever happens to the meek people is that they're trampled on and taken advantage of."

I sat up and swung my feet over the edge of the bed. "Listen, Nancy," I continued heatedly, "I've been reading a book called *The Return of Bridey Murphy*. In this book, a woman believes that she's lived in another lifetime. It sounds way out, but it sure makes more sense to think that Craig, who never had a real chance at this life, could return to have another shot at it."

"Brother, if your father could hear you now!" exclaimed Nancy. "I think you're just upset over this whole thing."

"Upset? Sure, I'm upset! Look, somewhere in the Book of Matthew, Jesus tells people they have to be perfect as their Father in heaven is perfect. How many people are perfect when they die? Yet most Christians just assume that if they lead a good life with a few sins here and there, they'll get into heaven anyway."

"Marti, you're forgetting a little thing known as forgiveness. If you are truly sorry for all the bad things you did in your life, Christ says you can be forgiven and get into heaven," Nancy retaliated as she began undressing.

"I can't buy that. Take a look at some of the very sinful people in our society. The ones with all the money they got from stealing from someone else. You mean you actually believe that if someone like Baby Face Nelson had truly felt sorry for all he'd done in his lifetime, God would have forgiven him and he would have gone to heaven alongside the poor Christian man he might have beaten to death? There would be no justice in that!"

"Never argue politics or religion," murmured Nancy as she headed toward the door, effectively ending our discussion.

In the morning, still troubled, I visited the Odoms, Pat's family. I thought they were doing remarkably well, and decided I should try to follow their example.

The day passed quickly and it was soon time for dinner with the Carellis. After dinner we went to the Lettermen's concert, and it proved to be as exciting as anticipated. Soon after it was over, we returned to my dormitory and said our goodnights.

"Linda, we'll be by to pick you up in the morning," said Mrs. Carelli. "Have a good time." Linda and I went to my room and chatted before going to bed, but not for too long because we knew the next day would be a very strenuous one.

Shortly after the alarm went off next morning, Terry, one of the cheerleaders, bounced into my room.

"Marti, we have the crepe paper and all the materials to start decorating the car whenever you're ready," she said.

"Good," I answered as I pulled on my sweatshirt and turned to Linda. "Ready to help? It won't take too long and will pass the time until your folks come for you."

"Let's go," answered Linda, and we headed out after Terry.

With the help of the rest of the cheerleaders, the car was decorated by the time the Carellis came to get Linda. As Terry and I were cleaning up the mess, she turned to me and said, "Guess who'll be riding in the car behind us today in the parade?"

"Who?"

"The Lettermen, would you believe it? They decided to stay over for the game and agreed to ride in the parade this afternoon!"

"Well, we've got to take the car over to the line-up now so maybe we'll run into them. Let's go," I said, and we piled into Terry's new convertible. Sure enough, when we pulled up before the gymnasium, we saw two of the Lettermen in their car.

"Hi!" I said to the blond one called Tony. "I sure did enjoy your concert last night."

"It was our pleasure. We enjoyed doing it," he answered with a smile. Several girls walked up to them and began taking pictures. Tony pulled me into the car, saying, "We need a few women to brighten up these pictures." With that he put his arm around my shoulder.

"You'd better watch your step! That girl is pinned to the captain of the football team," an unknown observer informed him.

"That only makes it more interesting," he commented as he kissed me on the cheek. "How about getting away from all this for a while?"

I grinned, flattered, but knew when to say no. "Terry and I don't have too much time. We have to change into our uniforms in about twenty minutes," I prevaricated.

"Well then, tell me what you think of the girls we've been fixed up with for the game tonight."

"Who are they?"

"Barbara Zobel and Nancy Settlemyre."

"They're both sorority sisters of mine and I'm sure you'll have a good time," I said sincerely. "We must be going. I'll look for you at the game tonight and afterwards we can all go out together somewhere. Hyski would be happy to meet you."

"Imagine, actually talking to the Lettermen!" Terry said excitedly as we headed back to the dorm.

"Yeah, I enjoyed it too, but right now I'm nervous thinking about the game tonight. It won't be an easy one to win," I replied, and went to my room to change.

The parade was a tremendous success, and tension was high over the entire campus. The field lights came on and people piled into the stadium to see the Lenoir Rhyne Bears take on the Appalachian Mountaineers. Since they were one of our biggest rivals, we could always count on an exciting game—and this one was no exception. The score at halftime glared from the scoreboard: 7-7!

The halftime ceremonies began with the presentation of the sponsors of the senior football players. I proudly walked out onto the field to represent Hyski. After the crowning of the Homecoming Queen, the football players returned amidst wild cheering from the fans. Once again, the battle was underway.

I barely had time to watch Hyski in action, for most of my attention was devoted to leading the crowds in the proper cheers. Both teams had scored again, but Lenoir Rhyne missed the extra point and the game entered the fourth and final quarter with Appalachian leading by one point.

Occasionally I glanced toward the stands. I saw Lettermen Tony and Jimmy with their dates, all of whom seemed to be enjoying themselves. I spotted the Carellis sitting on the fifty-yard line and knew they must be proud of the way Hyski was playing. Then the crowd began to roar as we intercepted a pass close to our goal line.

One of our players was injured on the play and I strained to see who it was, hoping it wasn't a starter. This season we had been plagued with knee injuries among our best football players, and already had three boys out for the season—including the co-captain.

"Who is it?" I asked Terry. "We ought to get a cheer underway for him."

"I don't know," she answered. I turned to several of the other girls, but they all seemed to be acting rather strangely.

"Beth, do you know who it is?"

"I believe it's Hyski," she answered solemnly. I looked toward the field and saw that the injured player still hadn't gotten up off the ground. My eyes searched the players for Number 58. Whenever a boy went down I always did that, but this one time, I had forgotten. Number 58 was not in sight. It had to be Hyski. When I looked for the Carellis in the stands, I could tell by their faces that my fears were justified.

Slowly, several managers and a doctor took the stretcher onto the field, and I saw Hyski refuse to get on it. He didn't want to be carried off the field, so with the help of two players, he hobbled toward the bench with his right leg dangling from the knee. My heart sank when I realized that it had to be torn cartilage and ligaments in his knee. In that brief moment, I realized what Hyski already knew. This game, the seventh of the season, was the last college game he would play.

I watched helplessly while they wrapped his knee. He refused to get into the ambulance, but remained on the sidelines until the game was over. We weren't able to score again, and Appalachian won 14-13. As the Alma Mater ended, I ran over to Hyski.

"Marti, get away from here!" he shouted thickly. Tears sprang to my eyes. When I turned away Tony was beside me.

"They're taking him to the hospital and I'm not letting you drive yourself. Come on, Nancy and I will go with you," he said firmly. Meanwhile, the Carellis had come down onto the field as the ambulance drove away with Hyski, its red light flashing. Linda ran over to me and cried, "Marti, what are we going to do?" Mr. and Mrs. Carelli, along with Uncle Howard didn't even try to hide their concern.

"What hospital will they take him to?" asked Mr. Carelli.

"It's not far from here, and Tony and Nancy have offered to drive me. You can follow us," I answered.

Once we got there, it seemed like hours before we were able to see Hyski. Then a nurse approached our small group.

"You may go in for a short while. The doctor says they'll be moving him tonight to Charlotte Memorial Hospital, since they'll operate on his knee in the morning," she said, leading us down a narrow hallway.

As I entered the room, I saw Hyski lying on a table, a slit in the side of his uniform, his knee and leg covered with bandages.

"Hi, hon. Are you doing okay?" I asked as he unsuccessfully tried to smile.

"Sure. Why didn't you ride with me in the ambulance?" he said, taking my hand. I knew then that he didn't remember adamantly refusing my company.

"I didn't think you wanted to be bothered, so Tony and Nancy drove me here. By the way, this is Tony, one of the Lettermen. We were going to double-date with them tonight."

"It's good to meet you, Tony. Your group has the perfect sound," Hyski murmured as his eyelids began to close. Obviously, the sedative they'd given him was beginning to take effect. Quickly, Hyski's parents told him they'd be leaving in the morning but would keep in close contact. Mr. Carelli turned to me.

"Take care of him for us and let us know if he needs anything. It was nice meeting you." And with that farewell statement, he kissed me on the cheek. I was startled at the unexpected affection and turned to see if Hyski had seen it.

"I told you they'd like you, Marti. I don't remember my father ever kissing any of my other girlfriends," he said, and fell asleep. I gently bent over, kissed him on the forehead and left the room.

The next day, Sunday, Hyski was operated on and the doctors termed it "very successful." During the next few weeks, I made several trips to Charlotte to visit Hyski. His spirits were lower than usual the day I went to bring him back to school.

"It sure has been hard just sitting here in the hospital while the boys continued playing football." He put his crutches under his arms and hobbled out of the room. "Oh, I appreciate the message you sent to me over the radio from Louisiana at the last game, even though I didn't get to hear it," he said as we took the elevator to the first floor.

"How come you missed it?" I asked, puzzled.

"For some reason, I couldn't breathe that night and I was rushed to the oxygen room. One of the student nurses heard the message over my radio and told me about it when I got back. I sure felt bad that night."

"We didn't have much chance of winning the game with all the injuries we had, but I think everyone enjoyed the trip except me. It was terribly lonesome without you on the field," I said, stretching out my arm to steady him as he clumsily went through the hospital's front door. I squeezed him around the waist. "You're going to have to practice some before you'll be able to tear down the corridors of the school buildings."

"Wasn't the thirtieth your twenty-first birthday?" he questioned, changing the subject.

"Yes, and we were flying over the Mississippi River when everyone sang *Happy Birthday* to me."

"I'm sorry I missed it, but we'll celebrate when I can get around a little better. The least I can do, though, is give you a birthday kiss," and he pulled me to him. I was startled to feel how much weight he had lost.

"How much do you weigh?" I asked.

"About a hundred and eighty-nine," he said with a laugh.

"One hundred eighty-nine pounds! That's a far cry from the two twenty-five you weighed a few weeks ago," I exclaimed. "We'll just have to fatten you up when you get back to school." I helped him into the car, got behind the wheel and took off for Hickory. "I hope this is our last sight of a hospital for a long time!"

But my hopes were soon dashed. One night, as Hyski and I were watching television in the lounge, he began having serious trouble breathing. He was rushed to the hospital and the diagnosis was a blood clot in his lung resulting from his knee operation. For several days, he was under complete sedation while those of us who loved him prayed that he would pull through.

Finally, a week after the incident, the clot dissolved and he began to recuperate. By Christmas, he was back to his normal self, and the new year began with the promise of a bright future together.

CHAPTER SEVEN

April, 1965

Spring was in the air. I could smell it all around me, giving me a sense of exhilaration, as I stepped out into the cool night. I glowed inside as I sat down on the dormitory steps to wait for Hyski to arrive. Since Christmas, time had flown and in another month, we would be graduating. It just did not seem possible that four years of college could have swept by so swiftly! But it had. Now we were facing the world on our own.

As I sat thinking about what Hyski had said the week before about getting married after graduation, the lounge door opened and Barbara, my suite-mate, stepped out onto the porch. She was smiling and sniffing the night air. I could tell spring was getting to her too when she said, "What a beautiful night! Doesn't it make you feel like forgetting about studying for final exams?"

"Yes, and I'm doing just that! Hyski went to see his parish priest about our getting married after graduation," I said with a sigh of anticipation.

"What is your father going to say about you marrying a Catholic?" Barbara asked as she sat down beside me and leisurely placed her elbows on her knees.

"No problem. Hyski promised me that Dad could marry us, so I guess he intends to marry outside his church," I answered and stood up to stretch my back. "I wish he'd get here soon. I don't want to waste such a lovely evening."

"I thought Hyski was a pretty good Catholic," Barbara said, surprised. "I'm from a Catholic community and I know if a Catholic marries outside his church, he's excommunicated. That means he's unable to partake of the Sacrament of Mass, which is a pretty big deal." Barbara stood up and proceeded toward the door. "I hate to do this to myself, but I have to hit the books. See you later."

Restlessly, I paced back and forth on the porch, wondering what my father would say if he got the idea I wanted to be married in the Catholic church. Just thinking about it made me shudder! I pushed the idea from my mind as Hyski drove up in his new car, a graduation present from his family. I ran down the steps to meet him.

"Let's take a walk tonight! It's such a beautiful evening!" I exclaimed as I bent through the car window and kissed him lightly on his forehead.

"I want to take a drive. Get in, Marti," he said soberly. With those words, I sensed that something was wrong and went around the back of the car to get in. After driving for a while, he opened the conversation. "Where are you planning to teach next year?"

"I don't know. I was offered a job in Statesville where you'll be teaching, and if we get married that's where I'll teach too. But if we don't get married, I can't see teaching in the same school system. It would be too complicated," I answered. "I haven't had that many job offers yet, and the ones I have had, I don't much care for, even the one in Statesville. Why do you ask?"

"I just wondered. We haven't seriously discussed what we were going to do after graduation and I think it's about time we did." He pulled the car to a stop in a wooded area near the college. "Does your father have to marry us?" he asked quietly.

So that was the crux of the matter. I thought for a few moments before answering, then said, "I'm the oldest and it would crush my father if he wasn't able to marry me. Yes, he must marry us."

"As you know, I talked with Father O'Hara tonight. If that's your final decision, then we can't ever get married," he said, and turned to look at me with anguish in his eyes.

"Are you saying you don't love me enough to let my father marry us?" I couldn't believe what I was hearing.

"You know I love you more than anyone, but I also love my church. Father O'Hara put a question to me tonight. He said, 'Al, are you willing to give up your eternal life by marrying outside the church?' When he asked me that question, I knew I couldn't do it." He took my hands in his.

"This is crazy," I said flatly. "You mean to tell me there's no way my father can marry us with the Catholic church's approval?"

"That's right. I know how much it means to you to have your father marry you, but won't you consider getting married in my church?"

I felt the tears spring to my eyes. "Hyski, are you telling me that unless we get married in your church you won't marry me—ever?"

"I can't. Don't you understand that I do love you, but I love God more and I could never leave my church."

I understood all too well what he had just said. The hurt of it all crept through my being and made me want to scream. I turned the door handle, jumped out of the car and ran through the woods. All I knew was that I wanted to run from what Hyski had said. I wanted to get away from him and cry it out of my system. As I ran, I was unaware of the slapping branches and nagging thorns. I didn't even feel my ankle twist when I caught it beneath the root of a tree and the ground seemed to come up and meet me. The cool earth on my face was like a comforting soul, enabling me to release my pent-up emotions. My body shook with sobs as I felt Hyski bend down beside me and take me into his arms.

"Marti, Marti, the last thing I wanted to do was to hurt you. I love you so much. Please, believe me, honey," he said as he cradled me in his arms.

"Hyski, I love you too. Please, let's not call it quits yet. Let me have time to think this through." I sat up and began to straighten my clothes.

"You look a mess!" he exclaimed. "You've even scratched your face." He took out his handkerchief and began to wipe the dirt and tears away.

"I'm sorry. I feel like a fool. I don't know what got into me. All I know is that I love you and want to marry you. Take me back to the dorm...I want to have time to think," I said and he helped me to my feet.

We walked slowly back to the car, arm in arm. On the drive back, I nestled my head on his shoulder, his arm around me pulling me close. It was quiet, each of us left with our own thoughts. As we pulled up in the back of Schaeffer Hall, he turned to me and asked, "Will I see you tomorrow?"

"Of course," I answered. "Why don't we meet for breakfast at eight?"

"Okay. Don't forget."

"Forget what?" I asked.

"That I love you." And he kissed me goodnight.

I walked to the front door, and luckily didn't meet anyone. At the moment, I didn't want to have to answer any unnecessary questions about my disheveled appearance. Quietly, I crept down the hall and went into my room.

"God! You look like hell warmed over!" Nancy shouted as I walked through the door.

"No questions, please. I don't feel like talking right now." I went to the bathroom to clean up. After getting ready for bed, I sat down at my desk and reviewed in my mind all that had happened that night.

"I just wish I could forget what my father would say about it all and think about how I'd feel if there was no father to worry about," I thought to myself, and slowly realized that I didn't know how I felt about it at all. I just didn't know enough about the Catholic faith.

The past year, I hadn't been sure about much when it came to God. I did know that I was very impressed with Hyski's faith. I knew he meant every word he had said that evening about not getting married if it would interfere with his religion.

I decided to write some of my feelings down. I hadn't written much poetry lately, but when I did I always felt better afterwards. So I pulled pen and paper toward me and began. It was early morning by the time I finished my composition. I crawled into bed, set the alarm and fell asleep.

It seemed like only minutes later when the alarm jarred me awake. Quickly I dressed, picked up my poem and headed toward the dining hall. Hyski was waiting at an end table. When he saw me come through the cafeteria line, he waved me over.

"Hi! Feel any better this morning?" he asked as I pulled up a chair beside him.

"I thought about a lot of things last night and have come to several conclusions," I answered. "About feeling better—I do."

"If you feel like it, let's talk," he said as he began digging into his eggs and bacon. "Yuk, they're still serving the same old stuff. You should feel honored that I got out of my warm, comfortable bed in order to be poisoned by the college cooks." He grinned tentatively.

"You should complain. When you're hungry, you eat!" I answered, then got down to business. "Listen, I've decided there must be a way for us to work things out. First, I want to take some instruction in the Catholic faith. I want to know as much as I can about what you believe in so strongly. And since there are only a few weeks of school left, I've got to make a decision about where I'm going to teach. I've decided not to take any of the jobs offered to me so far, but to apply for an opening position at Susquehanna University. It'll be a long shot, but I think it would be best for us to be apart for the next year."

"Will you want to give my pin back?" Hyski asked.

"Not unless you want it. I'm not planning to be away so I can date. I already know what I want—YOU. A separation would only give us an additional test." I had spent many long hours the past night thinking this out. "I don't think we should rush into an interfaith marriage—after all, your church specifies no divorce." With that said, I began eating my cold pancakes.

"Okay," he answered slowly, "but don't think it's going to be easy, because it won't be. Maybe...maybe it'll be good for both of us. We could probably even save some money," he added in an attempt to look on the bright side.

"Don't laugh, but I wrote something for you last night," I said. I took the poem from my Ed. 2 book and handed it to him.

"I didn't know you wrote poetry. You never cease to amaze me." Intently, he began to read.

LAMENTABLE VERITY

Soft are the whispers of the spring winds
Caressing the newborn leaves and flowers
As they laugh, playing hide 'n' seek
With those lovers who stroll down their paths.

In the radiance of the shining sun
And amidst the magnitude of the azure sky
The friendly flowers sense the happiness or sadness
Of those who pass them by.

Sleepily they snuggle close together
As the warm rays of the sun
Withdraw into the overshadowed sky
Leaving behind scattered tranquility.

From beyond this sleepy hollow one can hear
Lighthearted laughs echoing from within the still darkness
Yet beneath the moonlit shadows of the searching pines
Can be seen a girl and boy strolling hand in hand.

Toward the sacred dwelling of the flowers
They slowly wander.
As they near—oblivious to all but the wonder of their love,
Dancing shadows reveal two radiant faces.

In the midst of this solitude
They stop—face each other—embrace
Their smiling eyes become sober.

To one another they cling,
Grasping for this moment filled with
Happiness, security, oneness
Time be forever gone!

But time is reality
Only slipping beneath tightened fingers,
Leaving the two
Engulfed in pain and heartache.

As the flowers once more drowsily fall into slumber
A sigh is heard;
For this story can only be told
By the flowers asleep.

"Marti, that's beautiful! Thank you," Hyski said as he kissed my hand.

"It's not all that great, honey, but if you like it that's all that matters, because I wrote it for you." I squeezed his hand in return.

After that trying night, things seemed to return to a more normal routine. Exams passed smoothly for both of us, and graduation was upon us before we knew it. That day we both proudly walked onto the auditorium stage and received our well-deserved diplomas. Hyski was anxious to begin his first coaching year at Statesville High School, and I was elated over my acceptance as a physical education and health instructor at Susquehanna University in Pennsylvania. Hopefully, the next year would dissolve all doubts about our relationship and bring us together in Statesville as man and wife. With this foremost in our minds and hearts, we parted for one year.

CHAPTER EIGHT

September, 1965

Shrilly, the whistle sounded. "Okay, girls, enough running for today. Break into groups and begin individual skills. I'll be around to check you in a few minutes," I shouted. Turning, I headed toward the side of the field to pick up some extra field hockey pucks.

I was tired and there was at least another hour of practice left. My first month at Susquehanna University had proved to be very challenging, although I had a light schedule with my last class ending on Thursday afternoon. Aside from coaching the girls' field hockey team and the cheerleaders, I had no other outside duties.

I found that most of my students were my age or a year older, and often I wished that I had at least a year of teaching under my belt. With that experience, I felt, I could have been doing a better job.

"Miss B., which group do you want me to work with today?" asked Fran, a senior student who helped me with the coaching duties.

"Take the first three groups. I can manage the rest," I answered. I didn't know what I would have done without Fran's help. My knowledge of field hockey had been zip until I arrived and found out I would be coaching the team.

Slowly, I turned and rejoined the group. The remainder of practice went quickly. The girls had taken their showers and were heading back to their respective dorms when Fran approached me.

"What are you planning to do this weekend, Miss B.?"

"I hadn't thought about it. Why?"

"We're having a party tomorrow night and thought you might like to join us," she offered.

"Thanks for asking, but I'd better not." I felt it was best to keep the student-teacher relationship just that, although doing so had become the most difficult part of my job. Since I was so close to my students in age, I still enjoyed doing the same things they did. I was constantly being asked to join them, but so far had avoided it.

That made for a rather lonely existence for me, because most of the faculty members were at least fifteen years older than I was. I still hadn't met anyone my own age who wasn't a student. If it hadn't been for several aunts and uncles who lived in the area, I would have gone bananas. When times became unbearable, I was always welcome in their homes, and more than once this had been my salvation.

As I locked up the girls' side of the gymnasium, I thought about Hyski. He was probably still on the field practicing with the football team. I had given up on ever hearing from him through letters; I still had not received my first one. Instead we used a more expensive form of communication: every Sunday evening we talked on the phone for an hour or more, but even that didn't ease my loneliness. We were planning to meet at his home in New Jersey for Thanksgiving. Although it was already mid-October, Thanksgiving seemed a long way off.

As I got into the car, the thought of spending another weekend in my apartment alone was overwhelming. It was then that I decided to make a surprise visit to Hyski in Statesville. If I hurried I could leave within the hour, making North Carolina by early morning. I could have all day Friday to sleep while he was teaching school, and would be able to watch the football game that night. If I left early Sunday morning, I could still make Pennsylvania in time for a good night's sleep. My decision made, I headed excitedly toward my apartment.

The drive to North Carolina was long and tiresome, but my excitement kept me going. I turned the corner onto the street where Hyski lived at about four-thirty a.m., and to my surprise saw a light shining from his apartment window. Quietly, I parked the car and tiptoed to his window. As I peered through the glass, I saw Hyski bent over his desk. It was hard for me to believe that he was still working, for in about three hours he would have to be going to school.

Since his apartment adjoined the main house where his landlords were asleep, I had to be careful not to wake anyone. I tapped lightly on the windowpane. My first tap went unheeded. I tapped again and saw Hyski look toward the window. Cautiously he stood up, came over to the window, and peered out. When he recognized me, he gave a chuckle and went to the door to let me in.

"I might have known it was you, you nut! Who else would be tapping at my window at four-thirty in the morning?" he exclaimed as he held me close.

"Hi, hon. Were you surprised to see me?" I remained in his embrace, savoring every moment of his closeness.

"Surprised and happy to see you," he answered. "You're crazy for driving all night alone. You never know what might happen on some of those desolate roads."

"Never mind all that. I'm here and I want to know what you're doing up so late. Don't you have school tomorrow?"

"That's what I'm doing—preparing for tomorrow's World History class. With football practices and meetings, I'm never able to get to my lesson planning until late at night. I won't be able to keep up this pace much longer, either."

"I should say not! If you want to get any sleep, you'd better get it now. Tomorrow I'll grade some of the test papers I see lying over there. That should help you some," I said.

Together we shared his small single bed. Nestled close to him, I felt the security of his embrace and was soon in a deep sleep.

When I awakened, Hyski was gone, and on his pillow beside me was a note saying he would return after school. I looked at his clock. It was twelve-thirty p.m. Lazily, I showered and dressed, and began to grade the stack of papers piled on his desk.

Promptly at four p.m., he arrived. "I've made arrangements for you to attend tonight's game with the other coaches' wives. I'm sure you'll all get along."

"Okay. I'll see you afterwards," I said as he hurriedly left for the gymnasium.

The game that evening was exciting and Statesville won by a touchdown. I thought Hyski looked quite handsome as a coach, and he seemed to be very much in command of himself for his first season.

Time flew by, and too soon the weekend was over. It was stimulating to have been with him after our separation. With renewed vigor, and very anxious for the Thanksgiving holidays to come, I headed back to Pennsylvania.

CHAPTER NINE

December, 1965

I left the priest's parish house in a turmoil. I had been taking instruction in the Catholic faith for several months, but after today's session, I was certain that I could never accept their teachings. All along I had been telling Hyski not to worry, that everything would work out. At present, I was not so sure.

Slowly, I wound my car down the narrow streets and into the parking lot beside my row-house apartment. As I opened the car door, the cold crept through my heavy coat and sent me running to my front door. The warmth I felt as I entered my living room seemed to help little. As I opened the closet door to hang up my coat, I glanced at the travel posters lining the walls of my living room and thought how great it would be if I were in Paris or Spain. Living alone was beginning to get to me. It was Thursday evening, and I was faced with another long weekend and nowhere to go. Fortunately, for sanity's sake, I was able to make a trip somewhere on most of my free weekends.

I threw two frozen chicken pies into the oven, thinking about the lovely Thanksgiving weekend I had spent with Hyski at his home in New Jersey. It had been a wonderful time, but had passed too quickly. He was planning to fly down to Florida for Christmas to be with me at my home over the holidays. It seemed like all we ever did was to wait for some holiday so we could get together again. "But whose fault was that?" I commented aloud, turning to go into the bedroom.

As I sat on the bed changing clothes, I heard the commode flush upstairs. It was about the only thing I could ever hear to indicate that someone lived there. The apartment above mine was occupied by Jay, a forty-year-old bachelor. Whenever I needed anything, from a vacuum cleaner to a recipe, he was always there, ready to help. Even though he taught at the university, I never saw him unless he was coming or going from his upstairs apartment. There had been several occasions when, unthinking, I had run up the steps to borrow something and had become an unwelcome intruder on a candlelit dinner for two. He would then explain to his latest girl that I was the youngster who lived downstairs.

An odor was coming from the kitchen. "Oh, hell!" I shouted at the bedroom walls and ran to survey the damage. Fortunately, the potpies were still edible—just a little black around the edges. Just as I was ready to dig into the mess I called supper, the phone rang.

"Hello," I answered.

"Hi, Marti. It's Sam."

"What are you doing in town? I thought you were going to see your girlfriend this weekend."

"No, last minute changes. I thought if you could use the company, I'd come over this evening," he replied.

"I'd love it. I'm tired of looking at four walls."

"Okay. I'll be over when I can get there. Bye," he said and hung up.

Sam was the second person I met after moving here. He went to school and helped coach football at the university. He had played there for four years as a quarterback and decided to change his major to education so he could coach football in high school; hence his fifth year of college.

Sam was almost six feet tall, with a slender build, black hair and blue eyes. We officially met the day we were registering freshmen. He was assigned next to me, and we seemed to get along from the start. Our paths ran parallel, for he was a Lutheran with a Catholic girlfriend—we had the same problem in reverse. There had been many times when we chatted about our difficulties over a beer.

I returned to my supper. After clearing away the few dishes, I decided to call Hyski. I wanted to hear his opinion about what the priest and I had discussed today. Even though it was not Sunday, I hoped he'd be home to receive my call.

"Hello," came the landlord's voice.

"Hi, this is Marti. Is Al Carelli there?"

"Just a minute, please. He just got in a few minutes ago."

"Marti, what are you doing calling on a Thursday?" Hyski asked when he picked up the receiver.

"I just wanted to talk with you. It's so lonesome up here in bear country."

"It's lonesome here too."

"I've been going to my instruction every week, but today didn't go so well," I said.

"What do you mean?"

"Well, we got onto the subject of sex and all it entails. The priest and I didn't agree at all. In fact, he got right irritated with me. I know I'm not going to these classes to convert, but to learn, and I shouldn't always debate everything he says, but I can't keep my mouth shut," I answered.

"Be more specific. You sound like you're getting upset."

"Well, I am upset about it. It all started when he said the main purpose of marriage is having children, and I didn't agree. Then we got onto birth control and it went from there. I was so frustrated because he didn't seem to understand my side of it," I concluded in a husky voice.

"Don't start crying about it. The priest doesn't take all sides as you see it. For him there are no sides, it's just black and white as it is stated in the Bible. The Protestants seem to take things from the Bible and then twist them around until they fit their purposes. You have to try and understand," he said.

"I don't know if I'll ever understand," I cried.

"Look, Marti, this is getting us nowhere. Do you want to call everything off?"

"No, I don't, but I don't know if I can raise my children in your faith and that's the whole point, I suppose."

"I don't see how you'll ever change your mind. We had best go our separate ways now, before we get more involved and it becomes harder to part," Hyski said in a quiet voice.

"You really mean that?" I asked, feeling more misunderstood than ever.

"Look, I'm just tired of you always changing your mind! I thought at Thanksgiving you'd made up your mind about what you were going to do. I had planned on a summer wedding and now you're telling me you won't be able to live up to the idea of raising our children in my faith. Marti, the way I see it, we should go our separate ways."

Everything seemed so confusing. I could not comprehend what was being said and cursed the telephone for being such an inadequate means of communication. "Okay," I answered, my voice shaking.

"Don't cry. Look, I understand how you feel, and I don't blame you. I can't change my beliefs, and I never wanted to change yours. I only hoped you'd understand my faith enough to let our children practice it. Marti, we're both intelligent enough to know that if we can't solve this problem before marriage, then it won't be solved after marriage. The wisest thing for us to do is to start over by ending our relationship now," he said in a weary tone.

"All right, Hyski," I said numbly. "Take care." I was ready to hang up the phone when he added, "I want you to write my parents sometime this week to explain to them what's happened, if you don't mind."

"I will," I answered.

"Goodbye, then."

"Bye," I echoed and hung up the telephone. When I realized what had started out to be a conversation to ease my loneliness had turned out to be the end of a relationship, I relieved my emotions by crying stormily.

Minutes later, there was a knock at the door. Hurriedly, I wiped my eyes and went to open it. When I saw Sam standing there, I burst into tears again. It was a relief to have someone to talk to. After I explained everything that had happened, he said, "Don't worry. This will all clear up and you'll be back together before you know it."

"No, Sam, it won't. That's why it's so hard."

"Let's go to the movies," he suggested, lightly touching my cheek.

"Why not?" Together we left, and it felt good to have someone holding my hand.

For the next few days I saw a lot of Sam, but being with someone else didn't erase the emptiness I felt. Almost every moment of the day, my mind returned to Hyski.

CHAPTER TEN

December, 1965

I closed the door with my elbow and dropped my books on the desk. It had been a long day. My lectures had been boring and the students correspondingly restless. I couldn't keep my mind on my work, and several times had lapsed into complete silence in the middle of a sentence.

As I bent over to pick up a book that had fallen to the floor, I glanced at the empty space on my desk where Hyski's picture had stood. Like a flood, the tears came again. I had never felt so lost before. It was not as if this was the first time I'd ever broken off a relationship. Each time, I had felt bad, but in no time, it all passed. This was definitely different. No one I dated could make me forget Hyski.

I put my books away, turned on the radio to a romantic station, curled up on the couch, and began to mull over the events of the past two weeks. One fact was certain: I was truly in love for the first time in my life. In Hyski, I had found a combination of the traits I'd admired in different men I had dated. With me, he was always honest, sincere, generous, hardworking, courageous, loving and God-fearing. He showed a great respect for his family and friends, and in him I believed I had found the right man to complement my life.

Slowly I stretched out on the couch, and my mind returned to the conversation that had taken place the night before. In a depressed mood, I had called home to tell my father that Hyski and I had broken off our relationship because of religious conflicts. When I began to cry while talking to him, my father advised me to straighten out the differences if Hyski meant so much to me.

His reaction had taken me by surprise. I thought he would be pleased that we weren't getting married. For some reason, I felt I had betrayed him by falling in love with a Catholic boy. Not as a father, but as a minister, he had always advised me to marry a man of my own religious beliefs. Now, thinking back over our conversation, it came to me that subconsciously I had been afraid to hurt my father by going against his wishes. This unknown, deep-rooted feeling might have cost me the most important relationship of my life.

"Damn," I muttered and jumped up from the couch. As I crossed to my desk, a thought struck me. It was the answer to my problem—and seemed so simple that I couldn't understand why I hadn't grasped it months before!

I paced back and forth across the living room floor trying to straighten out the multitude of thoughts running through my brain. It was so clear. It wasn't a matter of which one of us was right or wrong; the simple truth was that we were both right. We both believed in God and that, by living a good Christian life, we could attain a lasting life with Him. It seemed rather insignificant that our different faiths had taught us conflicting ways to attain this specific end.

I felt so relieved by my revelation that I ran to the phone and dialed Hyski's number.

"Hello," answered a childish voice.

"May I please speak to Mr. Carelli?"

"One moment, please," came the polite response from the other end of the wire.

With my heart pounding and hands perspiring, I impatiently waited for him to answer.

"Yes? This is Al Carelli speaking."

"Hi! It's Marti," I exclaimed jubilantly.

"Hi," he answered, rather hesitantly. "What's on your mind?"

"The truth is that I've been just plain miserable and wanted to talk with you."

"It hasn't been any picnic for me either, but calling each other won't do either of us any good."

"There is really more to it than just a friendly conversation," I replied, and continued, "I talked with Dad last night and he made me see everything in a different perspective."

"How is that?"

"To be frank, he just told me to work things out between us—and that's what I did."

"Marti, you aren't making a whole lot of sense," he said with a sigh.

"Oh, Hyski, I hate to try to explain things over the telephone! If only I could come down this weekend and see you, but that's impossible. I have exams and then it'll be Christmas vacation. Would you reconsider and join me at my house as we planned before?" I asked.

"I just don't know. You've been up and down so much that I honestly don't know what to think."

"Please trust me. Look, I'll try to explain what happened and then you can decide whether a trip to Florida would be worthwhile." For the next thirty minutes, I pleaded my case.

"You really sound as if you believe what you're saying, but how am I to know you won't change your mind in the next two weeks and put us right back where we were before this conversation?" he asked.

"I suppose you don't know, but please try to trust me. It's so important that we ought to be willing to try at least once more," I said anxiously, realizing that he might very well turn me down.

"Okay, Marti, I'll meet you at Christmas and hope for the best."

"Great!" I answered, relieved. "I'll meet you on the twenty-third, and don't forget that I love you!"

I remained by the phone for several minutes savoring the contentment I felt. Christmas was around the corner, and I hoped it would be a turning point in my life.

PART TWO

CHAPTER ELEVEN

June 6, 1966

"Do you, Martha Elizabeth Bergstresser, take Albert Carl Carelli, Jr., to be your lawfully wedded husband, in sickness and in health, for richer or for poorer, for better or for worse, until death do you part?" asked Father O'Keefe.

"I do," came my husky reply.

"Before God and man, I now pronounce you man and wife. You may kiss the bride."

With hands clasped, we turned to one another. Gently, Hyski lifted my veil and softly kissed me upon the lips. Together we turned and retraced our steps down the aisle of the church as man and wife.

As we walked together, my thoughts returned to all that had led us to this moment, from our first meeting to Christmas six months ago. I remembered that Christmas so well.

****

For December, the weather was delightful. I met Hyski at the airport in my shorts and halter. It was rather comical seeing him walk off the plane with a heavy topcoat slung over his left arm.

"You certainly do look healthy," Hyski commented as he eyed my newly-acquired tan.

"Don't forget, I've been here a while and have a head start," I replied, looking up to receive his kiss. "Come on. Let's get your luggage and be on our way. We have a three-hour drive from here to Fort Myers."

The drive from Tampa to Fort Myers was pleasant, but neither of us spoke of what was uppermost in our minds. I sensed that he was taking it easy, that there was to be no rushing this time.

It was late when we arrived home and everyone seemed happy to see each other again. Before retiring for the night, Hyski approached me and said, "I know what's on your mind, but I still need time to think and feel things out. We'll talk it all out soon. Okay?"

"This is too important to be too hasty. You know how I feel about it, and I understand what you're feeling. It can't be easy for you to decide whether or not I've really made up my mind about this whole situation. After all, my past record hasn't been the greatest. When you're ready, we'll talk about it," I answered, more calmly than I felt.

As he went to his room, I wondered if these would be the last few days we'd ever spend together. In two days, it would be Christmas, and then we would be returning to our separate jobs. That night, the eve of Christmas Eve, I tossed and turned, my dreams playing havoc with reality.

On Christmas Eve morning, despite my restless night, I awoke with the excitement of Christmas in my veins. Quickly, I dressed and joined everyone in the kitchen for breakfast.

"Good morning. It's such a beautiful day!" I exclaimed as I stretched and inhaled the warm, salty air drifting in through the open windows.

"I just can't believe this is Christmas. Where's the snow and sub-zero weather?" asked Hyski as he came into the kitchen, sat down at the table, and began buttering his toast.

"I guess it does seem strange to you, but for us it would be different if we didn't spend this day at the beach like we've always done. I hope all this warm climate won't spoil Christmas for you," I said.

"No, I don't believe Christmas will be spoiled—but it'll take a while to get used to seeing a Christmas tree being gently blown by the warm breeze coming through open windows!"

Throughout breakfast, my brother and sisters were unusually quiet. When Hyski was about to leave the table, they all began talking at once.

"Al, would you play the piano for us?" they asked. Each of us had had our turns at learning to play, but only Rachel emerged with any ability. Even though we never mastered the instrument, we kept an old, beat-up piano in the Florida room and all of us enjoyed hearing someone else play it.

"Okay, let's go," he answered. I followed everyone into the other room, wishing it was that easy for me to get him to play.

He began with *A Summer Place*, and went from one song to another. When he started to get up, everyone asked him to play the *Boogie*, a piece he had composed himself. I knew if he played it, that would be the last one, because it took a lot of finger work and usually wore a blister on his index finger. As Hyski began to warm up, my brother Danny pulled out his tape recorder. Danny enjoyed trying to pick out songs on his own, mostly by ear, and he wanted a tape to listen to when Hyski left.

After Hyski finished the rousing number, Dad approached us. "Al, I must go over to the church and make sure everything is set up properly for this evening's services. Would you like to go along with me?"

My heart jumped into my throat. When I had arrived home, the first thing I did was tell my father about my decision to marry Hyski in the Catholic church, if he still wanted me. I explained it all to him as best I could. Nevertheless, I wasn't too sure that the two of them spending time together—in a church at that—was such a good idea.

"Sure!" came Hyski's reply and together they went out the door. While they were gone, the rest of us went to the beach.

When we returned, it was early evening and time to get ready for church. As everyone was madly dashing for the bathrooms, Dad and Hyski returned. Their simultaneous laughter could be heard as they approached the house—at least that was a good sign.

"Whoever is in my bathroom, clear out!" my father shouted as he pulled his newly-pressed black suit from its hanger and headed toward the bedroom. Hyski approached and gave me a crushing hug.

"Tonight we'll go to the early service at your church and to High Mass at mine, if that's agreeable to you," he said.

"Sounds good," I answered and retreated to the nearest room to get ready for the evening ahead. I felt good inside—I sensed that somehow the afternoon had turned out all right for Hyski and Dad.

After I got dressed, I stood in front of the Christmas tree waiting for the others, looking at the bright lights and bulbs, remembering when I was a child. It reminded me of the Christmas Eves of years ago, when my brother, sisters and I sat on the couch facing the tree, playing our very own special Christmas Eve game. We would choose our favorite bulb and stare at it until someone guessed which one it was. When the bulb had been found, it was someone else's turn to choose, and the game continued until it was time to leave for the Christmas Eve service.

I had just reached over to fondle one of my special bulbs that somehow miraculously had survived the years of packing and unpacking when Hyski came up behind me and encircled me with his arms. We stood this way for several minutes, each relishing our own thoughts.

"You smell good. What perfume are you wearing?" Hyski broke the silence.

"My favorite, White Shoulders."

"Marti, have you changed your mind about anything? Do you still think we can make it?" he asked from behind me.

"Yes, I know we can make it," I answered, still not turning around. Then, as Hyski's left hand came around my left side, I saw a flash of light.

"Will you marry me?" he asked, opening his hand to reveal a gold band with a shimmering diamond in it. The different-colored lights on the tree made the stone look red, blue, green and gold, while the warmth and excitement of the question filled my being. Turning, I faced him.

"I would be most proud to marry you, Hyski," I answered, still unable to believe our promise to marry had been exchanged. He lifted my left hand and placed the ring on my finger.

"I've had this ring ever since Thanksgiving—but until now, I wasn't sure you'd ever wear it," he said. "You have made me very happy!"

"Oh, Hyski, I only hope I'll be able to make you as happy as you've made me!" Wonderingly, I touched the ring.

****

We had reached the door of the church where our parents were waiting for us. I never asked Hyski what was said that day between him and my father, but apparently they had worked everything out. My father was here for the service and was reacting as any father of the bride would.

From the church we went out to brunch with all the relatives. After that, we said our goodbyes and headed toward Myrtle Beach for a four-and-one-half-day honeymoon...and the beginning of a four-and-one-half-year marriage.

CHAPTER TWELVE

February, 1967

I slowly pulled my 1965 navy blue Pontiac sedan into the driveway of our two-bedroom rented home. I turned off the ignition, reached for my school books and clumsily closed the car door with my right foot. Even though I had arrived at the doctor's office at three-thirty sharp, it was nearly five o'clock and I had to hurry to get supper on before Al returned home from school. I chuckled to myself as I fumbled through my pocketbook for the key to the front door. Dr. Mason had told me plainly that what was wrong with me wasn't my appendix as I had suspected, and had gently reprimanded me for diagnosing my own symptoms.

Finally succeeding in opening the door, I entered the house and was promptly greeted by Little Bit and Tiger, our two cats. One had been a reject found under the house, and the other a gift from a student. After piling my books on the dining room table, I crossed over into the kitchen in search of something to cook for dinner. As soon as I opened the refrigerator, I realized that today had been my grocery shopping day. Oh well, maybe Al would take me to dinner, I thought, and smiled.

We had been married for nine months and, except for one misunderstanding, all had run very smoothly. We both had our teaching jobs during the day and our respective coaching jobs in the evenings. As I left the kitchen to go into the bedroom, I glanced at the open door of the linen closet. The indentation of Al's fist was still clearly marked—the result of our one misunderstanding.

I laughed inwardly as I entered our average-sized bedroom, which was dwarfed by our oversized furniture. That one incident taught me not to keep feelings bottled up inside me, because now I knew they would eventually emerge. The longer you kept them in, the more forceful the eruption.

****

Looking back, our disagreement seemed rather slight. It happened after we had been married for about a month. Al was busy all day and night with his job and coaching preparations. Consequently, I was left alone with the housework.

The whole problem was that I was bored and hadn't met anyone my own age. This I conveniently blamed on Al, who married me and brought me to this situation. I moped around for days feeling sorry for myself, and then took a job working as a lifeguard during the weekdays and weekend nights. I'd prove to Al how lonesome it could be by being away on the weekends, the only time he had off. When I told him what I had done, I had never seen him so upset. In a burst of anger, he smashed the closest object, which happened to be the linen closet door.

Thinking his first reaction would be to ask me why I had done such a thing, I had been totally unprepared for his outburst of emotion and didn't know how to cope with it. Blindly, I ran out of the house and kept running until I had rid myself of my pent-up emotion. Fortunately, it was night—I don't think I would have had the nerve to go bursting out of the house like a lunatic in broad daylight.

After exhausting myself, I began walking home. As I reached our block, I saw Al getting into the car. I felt rather foolish and childish as I called to him that I was coming home.

He hugged me and said I had worried him by running off like that. Once we were in the house, he asked if I was unhappy being married to him. All I could do was cry, until finally everything I'd been feeling came out in a rush of garbled words. Al made me realize that all I had needed to do was tell him how I felt—that it hadn't been necessary to resort to such drastic measures to make him ask me what was wrong.

That was a whole new idea to me. For years I had been on my own, dealing with my problems by myself, never letting anyone else see me on the inside. Al made me realize that, when you are married, you need to be dependent on each other—total independence no longer exists. It was my first lesson in open communication, and I knew I would need much practice before I became an expert at it.

****

It had been a good lesson, I thought as I sauntered into the den, the last room of our five-room house. Actually, the room was to have been a second bedroom, but since it was paneled in pine, we converted it into a den. It would be relatively easy to remove the trophy case, bookcase, couch, chair and television and rearrange it into a nursery, I told myself as I placed my hands on my stomach.

Just as I looked at my watch and saw that it was five-thirty, Al walked into the living room.

"Hi, hon. What's for dinner?" He gave me a kiss.

"Well, when I got home from the doctor's, I realized I was out of food so I thought maybe you could find it in your heart to take me out to eat," I answered and smiled sheepishly.

"Do you have it?"

"Have what?" I asked.

"Do you have appendicitis like you thought?" He began opening the mail.

"No, but what about taking me out to dinner? And is there any mail for me?"

"No, on both counts!" he answered. "Do you mind very much? I'm tired, and we can always have soup and sandwiches."

So much for the atmosphere of candlelight and soft music, I thought to myself. "Would you consider taking me out to dinner if we had something to celebrate?"

"Depends on what we're going to celebrate."

"Hyski, you really are making this difficult!" I replied, slipping back to his nickname of college days.

"What in the world is on your mind, woman? Spit it out," he said with a laugh.

"All right, if I must. Come here." I led him into the den. "Look over in that corner where the bookcase is. Don't you think we could fit a crib in there? And a small dresser would go nicely where the trophy case is, and..."

"Wait just a minute!" Al broke in. "What in the world are you talking about all this for now?"

"Honey," I said, turning to face him, "what I thought was appendicitis turns out to be a four-week pregnancy! I know it's a surprise, but we'll be able to manage. I can finish out the year teaching, and—"

"Don't go so fast," he begged. "I'm not worried about managing financially. I'm really pleased. Just give me a minute to get used to the idea of almost being a father!" He took me into his arms. "Just think! Our first son."

"There's no guarantee it will be a boy. A girl will do, won't it?"

"Sure, honey. I'm just dreaming. About that dinner—aren't you ready yet?" He helped me into my coat, took my hand and opened the front door.

CHAPTER THIRTEEN

November, 1967

"And the extra point is—good! Statesville is now leading with three minutes left in the game. Sure looks like they'll now have an 11 and 0 season and be a big contender for the State Championship!" shouted the announcer over the loudspeaker. Excitedly, I sat my heavy body down on the hard wooden bleacher and turned to Donna Abercrombie, the head coach's wife.

"I still can't believe it! Eleven straight wins! I also can't believe I'm still coming to the games. This baby is taking its good time about getting here."

"Be patient. It's your first, and they're usually late," she said confidently.

"If anyone knows about these things, you should," I replied. "After all, you've experienced four births!"

"Nothing to it. Oh, it looks like the game is about over."

"Ten, nine, eight, seven, six, five, four, three, two, one, HURRAY!" roared the crowd as everyone rushed out onto the field to embrace their friends, boyfriends and children.

"I'm so happy they won!" I sighed. "Guess we might as well make our way over to the gym and wait for the fellows."

"Do you mind going by yourself? I've got to get home and fix the table so we'll have something to eat when everyone gets there."

"No, I'll go on over with Becky," I answered, and began searching the crowds for the assistant coach's wife. Spying her on the edge of the field, I shouted for her to wait.

"Have any labor pains yet?" Becky asked as I breathlessly walked up beside her.

"No—but at least I didn't have the dilemma of going to the hospital before or during the game. I'd be afraid to find out whether Al would have gone with me or not! I've always had visions of the sports announcer crying over the intercom that Coach Carelli had become a father during the second quarter," I said laughingly.

"One of the hazards of being in the profession," she answered. "Never have a baby during football season!"

Slowly, we made our way up the steep incline toward the gym. Cars were beginning to file out and the field was deserted again. About twenty minutes later, the men appeared, talking noisily among themselves.

"Hi, hon. Good game!" I said to Al as he approached, circled his arm around my shoulder and gave it a squeeze.

"Not bad," he answered, "but maybe not good enough to knock off next week's team. We'll really have to do some rallying to beat Hickory!"

As we started walking to Coach Abercrombie's house, Al confided, "You know, Marti, I really love coaching. It's not just the winning, but also the molding of boys into men. There are so many facets to coaching, and they're all challenging. I just wish I could do it on a full-time basis."

"That's funny. I thought you were doing it on a full-time basis!" I attempted a joke as we neared the brightly-lit ranch house.

"No. I'm torn between two careers. All day I'm in the classroom trying to teach World History, in the afternoons I'm coaching the boys, and at night I'm working on game preparations. There aren't enough hours in the day for it all. I'm afraid I'm neglecting my classroom duties, and that makes me very frustrated. You know me, I can't stand to do any job halfway!"

We reached the front door and were greeted by a cheerful Donna. "Come in, folks! I'll bet you're starving, as usual. The food is on the table, so help yourselves."

"You bet!" answered Al as he ushered me into the living area. I took off my coat and visited with the wives as the men gathered together to rehash the game and unwind. Since the mood was jovial, the evening passed swiftly and it was soon time to go home.

"Enjoyed it as much as ever," Al said. "But Marti's rather tired, so we'd best hit the road."

"Who? Me?" I yawned. "Guess I'm not much good for late hours these days." With our coats wrapped tightly around us, we went out into the cold November air. As we got into the car, I turned to Al and asked, "Were you really serious about wanting to just coach football and not teach?"

"Yes, I was." He turned the car down the narrow road toward the back of the gym.

"If you meant it, then why don't you do just that?" I asked, pulling my unbuttoned coat a little closer to my neck.

"It's not as easy as it sounds. First of all, about the only place you could devote all your energies to football is in college coaching, and there are hundreds of coaches like me trying to break into those ranks. Second, I'd need a Master's degree in case I had to teach a class or two. At the moment, neither seems close to becoming a reality." He sighed and brought the car to a halt in our driveway.

As we got out of the car and hurried into the warmth of our home, I continued to question him.

"Why can't you try to do both? If it's a Master's degree you need, why not get one?"

"Marti, if I started commuting in the spring and summer only, it would take me seven years to get a degree! By that time, I'd be too old to even contemplate a college coaching career," he answered as he went into the bedroom and began undressing.

"Okay, so get your degree in one solid year." I followed him into the bedroom and began unzipping my long-sleeved woolen maternity dress.

"How will we live? We're about to have a baby! Maybe if we didn't have any children, it could be possible," he answered from the bathroom.

"As far as I'm concerned, that's no major problem," I shouted to him from the bedroom as I struggled to get into the only nightgown that still fit comfortably over my oversized belly. "Look, I have my teaching degree. I can work while you devote your time to studying. It might even be possible for you to get some kind of graduate assistantship." I joined him at the bathroom sink and retrieved the oozing tube of toothpaste.

"I don't know. That would mean putting the baby in a nursery and you know how I feel about working mothers," he answered with a sigh and returned to the bedroom.

"Eh wou onli ee or a ittle ile," I muttered while toothpaste dribbled down my chin.

"For God's sake, how do you expect me to understand you? Finish brushing your teeth before you start talking again!" Al exclaimed from beneath the bedcovers.

"I said, 'It will only be for a little while'," distinctly pronouncing each word.

"All right, so what if I get my degree but no coaching job?"

"That's a chance you'll have to take. Besides, you might even want to work on your doctorate and stay in the teaching field. Either way, your Master's would be good to have. It looks like the only way to do it is all at once. With only one child, it'll be a lot easier than with two or three." I snuggled close to the warmth of his body.

"Well, I guess it wouldn't hurt if we applied at several different universities. The place I'd really like to attend is the University of North Carolina at Chapel Hill." Suddenly, Al seemed to make up his mind. "Okay, tomorrow I'll write out a list of universities where you can send out letters of application, and then we'll take it from there."

"Al, tomorrow I'd like to call the junior high school about a job in January. I know there's a physical education opening coming up. Would you mind terribly if I went back to work and saved the money just in case you do get to go back to school?" I asked rather hesitantly.

"Sure I'd mind. The baby isn't even here yet and already you're planning on leaving it!" he said, disgruntled.

"Honey, the baby is due tomorrow, and even if he's very late, I'd still be with him for at least two months before going back to work. Also, he'd be so young that he wouldn't know the difference. By the time he was old enough to realize I wasn't around, it'd be summer and I'd be home again."

"Let's just take one thing at a time. First, let's worry about getting accepted somewhere. Come on, it's four in the morning and we both need our sleep. It sure wouldn't do for you to be tired out if the baby should decide to come into this world today," he sighed, patting my bulging stomach and turning onto his side.

Obviously the subject was closed, but it certainly wouldn't hurt for me to get my name into the pot just in case I needed to go back to work.

"Don't forget Dad is driving Mom up tomorrow," I said. Placing my left leg on Al's side in order to equalize my stomach, I promptly fell asleep.

CHAPTER FOURTEEN

November 15, 1967

"While we're all sitting here, Mom, could you take a picture of me? I'd like to have one taken while I'm pregnant." I moved onto the couch and smoothed down my hair. My mother, who at forty-eight still retained a youthful beauty despite her slightly graying hair, went into the kitchen for the camera.

Returning, she said, "I suppose we ought to get this on film, since I doubt that your baby will be too much longer in coming."

"I wish I could believe it. I'm five days overdue and the doctor said this morning he thought it'd be at least another week. I'm getting rather discouraged," I complained, then smiled as the flash went off.

"Come on, Marti, cheer up. After all, I'm here to keep you company," said my brother Danny, who had just returned to the States after spending almost a year on the front lines in Vietnam.

"Okay...hmmmm!" I moaned as a lingering pain slowly spread from my back to my lower stomach and vanished.

"Was that a labor pain?" My mother quickly came over to me.

"It was something, and it definitely hurt. I thought the first ones were supposed to resemble cramps."

"I couldn't say, it's been so long since I've been in your situation, Marti, but you'd better start watching the clock just in case," my mother suggested.

"It's after ten o'clock. Maybe you should get ready for bed, lie down, and see what develops," Al said from the dining room table where he was grading test papers.

"I think I'll get some shut-eye, too." Danny yawned, stretched, and headed for the studio couch in the den.

"I'm going to lie down for a while, too, but I'll be ready if you need me,

Marti. If you do, just holler." Mom gathered together her magazines and retreated to the bathroom.

"Al, are you coming to bed, too?" I asked from the doorway of the bedroom.

"I'll be along in a minute. I just have a few more papers to go."

"Okay," I answered and began undressing. Just as I was about to climb under the covers, I felt the beginning of another pain. I looked at the clock, which read ten-thirty. Thirty minutes had elapsed between my first and second pain. Not remembering what the doctor had told me to do in this case, I went in search of the manual he'd given me at the start of my pregnancy.

"Aren't you in bed yet?" Al asked as he pushed his chair away from the table, gathered his graded papers together and neatly put them to one side.

"I just had another pain or contraction or whatever they're called and I'm looking for the little green book the doctor gave me several months ago," I answered, opening one drawer after another.

"Don't you imagine you probably put it in the bookcase somewhere?" Al tiptoed into the den so he wouldn't disturb Danny, and rooted through the bookcase.

Returning, he held up the small green book. "'*Expectant Motherhood,* by Dr. Dobson'," he read, and handed the copy to me.

"I sure wish I'd read this earlier. Do you know that I don't even know how to change a diaper? I guess I figured it would all come naturally." I flipped hurriedly to the section on labor. "Ah, here it is! 'When the pains are approximately five minutes apart, you should then proceed to the emergency room of the hospital if it is after closing hours at the office; otherwise, call the office for further instructions.'"

"How long is it supposed to take to get the pains from thirty minutes to five minutes apart?" Al asked, reading over my shoulder. Just at that moment, I experienced my third pain.

"What time is it now?" I asked. "I just had another one."

"It's now ten forty-five on the dot!" he answered, looking at his watch. "Maybe we ought to go to bed and count from in there." He led me to the bedroom.

After forty more minutes passed without a suggestion of a pain, I decided the doctor was probably right about it being another week, and turned out the light to get some sleep. Then, when I was quite drowsy, I felt the beginnings of another, more intense pain. This one lasted for almost a full minute. Turning the light on, I looked at the clock. It read eleven-thirty.

It was time, I decided, to take this more seriously. So, finding a piece of paper and pencil, I jotted down the time the pains occurred, checking beside each one if it was hard. So far, they had been definitely erratic, but certainly intense.

Al was sleeping soundly. I didn't disturb him, but turned on the light across the room, then climbed back into bed and patiently waited for the next pain to hit. By six o'clock the next morning, I had had little or no sleep. The pains had been irregular all night, but so intense that they kept me awake. The alarm woke Al at six-thirty.

"What are you doing awake, hon? Still having pains?" He reached over and picked up the white sheet of paper scribbled with a long line of figures. "You've had this many pains already?" he asked, concerned.

"Yes, but they're still so irregular," I answered bravely while another pain gripped me.

"Honey, if they hurt that much, shouldn't you call the doctor?" He came over to me and sat down on the edge of the bed.

"I don't know what to do. They're still between ten and thirty minutes apart and the manual says not to call until they're five minutes apart."

"What does the manual say about calling when it's your first baby?"

"It says to call whenever you're not sure of something," I admitted, "but I'm afraid to call if it isn't the real thing."

"Would you like me to stay home from school?"

"No, I'll call if I need you, and I promise to call the doctor when his office opens at ten this morning."

"Are you sure? All I have to do is call the school." He went to the closet looking for something to wear.

"I'll be all right. Mom is here to keep me company, and you can bet I'll let you know when it's time to take me to the hospital," I said, more bravely than I felt.

Soon everyone was up and dressed. I was in the kitchen, beginning to fix breakfast, when Mom popped in from around the corner of the hallway.

"Al told me what's been going on, and if you don't get back into bed, I'll have to resort to some pretty strong measures!" she scolded, shaking her finger at me.

"Mom, I'm worried. The pains are so hard. Did it hurt this much for you?" I asked, holding tightly to the counter top while still another pain ripped through my pelvic area.

"Honey, if you ask me, you're in labor, so get off your feet and let me get Danny and Al off to school. Danny's going in to talk with Al's classes about the war."

"Okay, but could you bring me a gigantic glass of water? I feel like I've been wandering over a desert all night, I'm so thirsty!"

At ten o'clock, I called the doctor, who told me I was probably in false labor since I had been having pains for twelve hours with no consistency. I was told to stay off my feet, and that if it was false labor, the pains would subside.

At noon, Al called to see how I was progressing. By four o'clock, the pains were still ten minutes apart but almost unbearable. When I spoke with the doctor again, he was at the hospital between deliveries. Hearing my frantic voice, he told me to come on to the hospital and bring my suitcase in case I needed to be admitted. When I called Al at school, he canceled basketball practice and came straight home.

"You aren't acting very nervous," I said as he drove me up the hill toward the hospital.

"Well, I am. I'll feel a lot better when this whole episode is over," he admitted as we drove into the hospital parking lot. Switching off the ignition, he turned to pick up my suitcase off the back seat.

"No! Don't take that thing in yet. What if I'm not in labor and I have to go back home? I'd certainly feel stupid then!"

"All right, but let's go," he said, and we entered the swinging doors of Iredell County Hospital. Immediately, I was taken to an examining room where Dr. Mason checked me.

"You are definitely in labor," he said, "but you have only dilated one centimeter."

"How many do I have to dilate to give birth?" I asked.

"Ten," he answered. "I'm sending you to X-ray. It looks like it might be a breech. Do you understand what that means?"

"Yes. The baby isn't head first as he should be," I answered apprehensively.

"We'll know more after we see the X-rays. Put on your gown, and someone will be down for you in a minute," he said and walked out of the room.

Once the X-rays were finished, I was taken to a room where Al was waiting for me. He was extremely pale and rocking from one foot to another.

"Are you feeling okay?" he asked, coming over to me and taking my hand.

"Yes," I lied. "What did you find out?" Pains racked my body yet again.

"It's feet first."

"Anything else?" I inquired. "You look so pale."

"That's all. The doctor's coming down the hall now and it looks like he wants me to leave." As Dr. Mason approached, Al wandered down the hall.

"Mrs. Carelli, it looks as if we have a definite breech on our hands. From the X-ray pictures, it seems that you have room to have a normal delivery, so no 'C' section is planned at this time. There is a room ready for you. How do you feel?" he asked, rather businesslike.

"Well," I said with a shrug of my shoulders, "it hurts."

"It will be quite some time before this baby is born, so try to relax between labor pains. I'll be down to see you after my next delivery," he said and hurried down the corridor. The nurse arrived, put me in a wheelchair and began wheeling me toward the elevator.

"Wait!" I yelled. "I see my husband. Can't I talk with him for a minute?"

"Okay. Just for a minute," the nurse answered and walked over to the nearest desk. Al came up and took my hand.

"I won't be able to see you again until after the baby is born," Al said, smiling at me.

"I wish you could be with me while I'm in labor."

"Don't worry, it'll soon be over. Besides, I'm to have company. Mom and Danny are on their way over," he said as the nurse left her station. "I love you," he whispered as she came up behind him.

"Me to you, too," I called from the elevator as the door slid shut.

It wasn't long before I was ready to go to the labor room, where I would stay until time for delivery. During the long hours of labor, I tried to distract myself by watching the clock overhead. By ten forty-five p.m., the pains had been coming one after another for hours.

"Nurse! Nurse!" I cried between contractions. The nurse came over, sponged my face and placed a damp cloth on my lips. "How much longer? I'm not having any time to rest and I don't know how much more I can stand." My breathing became harder.

"Let's take another look," she said softly. "Oh! I can see a foot!" Hurriedly, she called for the doctor. The next few minutes were rather hectic as I was moved onto a table and rolled into the delivery room. Since it was my first visit to a hospital, the appearance of the delivery room gave me a fright. There was a huge, bright light overhead and large iron stirrups for my feet.

"Just relax, Mrs. Carelli," Dr. Mason instructed. I looked up to see his mask-covered face at my feet. "We are going to need your cooperation. When I say push, I want you to push outward as hard as you can."

"I'll try," I answered, trying to muffle the moan beginning in my throat.

"Push! Push!" he said sternly from the end of the table.

"I am! I am!" A scream tore through my lips.

"The baby's shoulders are out! Damn it, put her to sleep!" the doctor shouted. As I sucked in the foul-smelling odor, all pain left me and a vision of the wall clock went through my mind. It read two minutes past eleven.

****

"Come on, wake up," someone was saying, slapping me lightly on either side of my face. Before opening my eyes, and without knowing how I knew, I said, "It's a boy and he weighs seven pounds, nine and one-half ounces."

"Right on the nose," answered Dr. Mason. I opened my eyes and saw my son for the first time, and he looked just like I thought a son of mine would look. I noticed how beautifully round and unmarked his head was.

"You were right, doctor, it was a boy. Just like you predicted," I murmured. "Thank you." Taking my hand, Dr. Mason gave it a gentle squeeze. Then he smiled, patted me on the shoulder, and left the room. I thought to myself that he wasn't as stern as he pretended to be.

"If you need anything, just push that button and someone will be here," said the nurse as she tucked the sheet securely under the mattress. As she left, she passed Al entering the room. He came over to the bed. With his tousled hair, wrinkled clothes, unshaven face and wide grin, he reminded me of a huge teddy bear. He bent down and gave me a kiss.

"Oh, honey! I am so proud! We have our Vincent, our firstborn son!" His eyes began to fill. It was the closest thing to a tear that I would ever see from him.

CHAPTER FIFTEEN

November, 1967

"Waah! Waah!" came the bellows from Vince's room. At first I thought I had been dreaming, but then realized the sound was the baby crying. I bounded out of bed and raced to his room. Groping for the light switch, I saw that my mother was already bending over his crib.

"I'll tend to him, Mom. You go on back to bed," I said and picked up my son. Flicking off the light, I headed for the kitchen and the formula. One week of these nightly journeys, and already I was exhausted.

"And how long is this to go on, young man?" I asked him while I plugged up his moans with a bottle. Looking at the clock, I noticed that it was just after two a.m. "Right on time, as usual!" I settled into Al's orange chair and plopped my feet on top of the brown hassock. As I sat there feeding our baby, my mind returned to the preceding day's events and my heart ached. Although it had all happened yesterday, I was still in a state of shock and found everything hard to believe—or did I?

****

I could still vividly remember my last visit home. It was in the early spring and I had flown home without Al. It seemed so long since I had last seen my parents, and being in the first months of pregnancy, I was homesick. When I entered the house I was introduced to our houseguest, Carol. As she came bouncing out of the kitchen, I noticed that she was rather tall, of medium build with long, sandy-colored hair. She was not outstandingly striking, and my interest in her vanished immediately after the introduction. It was not unusual for my parents to have a guest—they were always inviting people with problems into the parsonage.

As the days of my visit passed into a week I began taking more of an interest in Carol. I noticed that my mother was always waiting on her, and I began to resent her not doing her share of the work.

Carol had four children, but wasn't able to support them all. The Welfare Department had her three oldest in a boys' home; Brenda, her only daughter, was with her. My mother had met her through her job, and because she had no place to stay, invited her into their home until she could get back on her feet. As a minister, my father had taken an active interest in helping her get custody of her three boys.

Uneasily, I watched her flutter around the house, constantly flirting with my father. Right before I left to return to Statesville, I felt I had to bring the matter up with him.

"Dad, may I talk to you about something before I go?" I asked as he helped me put my suitcases into the car.

"Sure. What's on your mind?"

"I hope this won't sound ridiculous, but I have a feeling Carol is trying to steal you away from Mom."

"Don't be silly, Marti. She's just a very sensitive person who has a lot on her mind," he answered, rather matter-of-factly.

"I still don't like the way she behaves in your home. Half the time she acts as if Mother is her very own personal slave, and when Mom isn't home, she acts as if the place belongs to her," I retorted angrily.

"Look, don't worry about it. There's nothing going on between us. Come on, let's go before we're late." He closed the car doors.

"Okay, but just be careful. I don't trust her innocent ways," I replied as we backed out of the driveway and headed for the airport. As I kissed my father goodbye, I thought that I might have gravely misjudged Carol and dismissed all suspicious thoughts from my mind.

****

I glanced at the clock again and noticed that it was almost two forty-five a.m. Vince was finally finished with his early-morning bottle and I gently placed him in his crib, trying not to wake him. I hurried to bed in order to get some much-needed sleep before his next awakening at six. As I tossed and turned, my thoughts kept returning to the day before and sleep became impossible.

It had been a little after lunchtime when Mom received that devastating letter. It was short and to the point—my father had left my mother and gone off somewhere to live with Carol. The parsonage was deserted except for the furniture and packed boxes. My father had also formally left the church and his profession. The facts were that Mother had no money and no place to live. My oldest sister was still in college, my brother safely in the Marines and my youngest sister was living with a friend.

I had been totally shocked until I remembered my latent thoughts concerning Carol on my last visit home. I also thought about the silver platter that my brother and sisters and I had bought for our parents, a gift for their twenty-fifth wedding anniversary. We were going to surprise them with it when my father came to pick up my mother the next week.

When Al returned from school, I had told him the whole story. Since I was the oldest, I felt that the rest of my family was now my responsibility. We decided to think about what to do and to discuss our thoughts the next day.

Early the next morning, behind closed bedroom doors, we found an answer of sorts.

"Honey," Al said, as he began looping his tie, "I've thought about Mom's situation a lot and have come up with a solution, if you're agreeable."

"What's that?" I sighed and sat down on the bed. He came over and sat down beside me.

"Remember how, before we were married, we discussed what we would do if our parents ever needed our help?"

"Yes."

"Well, I know it's happened a lot sooner than either of us thought it would, but Mom has no place to go but here. I know we've made future plans, but maybe she could live here with us for the next six months. By then she might be on her feet enough that she could begin life over again on her own. What do you think?"

It was exactly what I was hoping he would say, and the tears sprang to my eyes. He put his arm around me and held me close while I finally let my feelings escape in a rush of sobbing.

"It's better to get it all out," he said and held me closer. When at last I recovered, I wiped my eyes and blew my nose on his clean handkerchief.

"Al, I'm so grateful to you for feeling this way. It's really the only solution to Mom's problem."

"It will be hardest on you, Marti. After all, you're the one who will be with Mom day in and day out, and I know it could become a strain for both of you. You haven't lived with your parents in so long that you'll be bound to have some conflicts."

He got up from the bed and headed toward the door. With his hand on the knob, he turned back and said, "If it was my mother, we'd do the same thing. I always want us to feel that we can take care of our parents if they ever need taking care of. Would you like to tell her?" I nodded, and with a kiss he went out of the room into the kitchen. As I pulled myself together, I heard him shout goodbye and close the front door.

"Morning, Mom," I said, entering the kitchen and beginning to clean up the dishes. I could tell she had been crying.

"Mom, Al and I have talked this whole thing over and we have a proposition to make you," I said as I brought my coffee and her hot tea to the kitchen table and sat down opposite her.

"I feel so terrible about this whole thing," she said, and wiped her eyes on a wrinkled handkerchief that she had been twisting between her fingers. "It just doesn't seem right that you and Al should have this problem thrust on you so soon after your marriage, but I just don't know who else to turn to." She blew her nose.

"Look, Mom, don't worry about a thing. We have it all figured out. First, we want you to just stay here and make this your home for a while. You'll be able to sleep in Vince's room with him, and when I start teaching in another month, we'll pay you to watch the baby. Okay?"

"I'll love watching my grandson, but I don't want you to pay me for doing it," she said emphatically.

"How else do you plan on getting money?" I asked. "After all, we'll have to pay someone to watch him, and I'd much rather it be my own mother!"

"I won't be able to stay here for too long," she muttered. "I should get back to Florida and be with your sister Becky."

"She seems to be happy staying with her friend in Fort Myers," I soothed, then had to bring the question out into the open. "Mom, how long have you known about Carol and Dad?"

"Several months," she answered in a low tone. "When I found out, your father was determined for us to make a go of it, so we moved to a new congregation in Miami. However, we weren't there for very long before Carol showed up and started bothering him again. When you asked me to come to be with you, I was certain that all was well between us, but I was wrong."

"Even though Al hasn't heard whether or not he's been accepted, we're still planning to leave Statesville so he can go back to school. We won't be moving for another six months, and by then you might have saved enough money to get back home," I gathered my thoughts and spoke practically. "Meanwhile, now that I've persuaded Al to let me go back to teaching, we need a babysitter. And Vince couldn't be happier about it being his grandmother."

As the conversation ended, a look of calm came over my mother's face. I knew that in some small way she had resigned herself to what had happened, and found comfort in knowing we were there to watch over her.

Within the next six months she obtained a job as a sales clerk, because the days with Vince left her too much time for reminiscing about days gone by. My mother eventually moved to an apartment, bought a car and saved her money to return to Florida. However, it was several years before she was able to begin a new happy life. Still ahead of her were many months of agonizing torments, lonely nights and heartbreaking decisions from which she would emerge a stronger individual.

Many years were to pass before I was able to understand and accept the decision my father had made in divorcing my mother and marrying Carol. As time has a way of doing, it proved a healer, allowing both my parents to find peace and happiness within their respective lives.

Chapter Sixteen

May, 1968

"Are you ready yet?" Al yelled to me from the bedroom.

"Just about," I answered. "I just have to put this stupid eyeliner on and then I'll be beautiful."

"I don't know why you bother with that stuff! You hardly ever wear it and I think that you look beautiful without it." He entered the bathroom and made a face at me in the mirror.

"I don't know why I bother either," I sighed, "but somehow I feel a little more dressed up with it on. Does it really look that bad?"

"No, it looks just fine," he said, in order to avoid a lengthy discussion on the matter.

"Ready? Let's go. We don't want to be late for your last Statesville Athletic Banquet!" I hurried into the living room, grabbed my coat and opened the front door. "Susan, you know where we'll be if you need us," I told our babysitter on the way out.

On the ride over to the school cafeteria, we discussed our moving plans for the hundredth time. The big move was only a few weeks away and we were very excited. Al had received a graduate assistantship in teaching from the University of North Carolina at Chapel Hill, but I knew he was disappointed that he hadn't heard anything about coaching football there instead.

I had also obtained a teaching position, forty miles from Chapel Hill. It wasn't the ideal situation, but I felt fortunate to have gotten it since there was such an extreme overabundance of teachers in that area. Our biggest headache had been finding appropriate housing, but we had just heard the day before that we could have an apartment in Odum Village, the university's student housing. The apartments were adequate and inexpensive, and we were both looking forward to living there in close contact with other graduate students our age.

Al pulled the car into the parking lot and helped me to the door of the cafeteria, where we ran into one of the other coaches and his wife, Tony and Becky McClamrock. They too would be moving soon. "Hi, Becky, Tony," we greeted them. "Anything interesting going on?"

"No, but the food looks good!" commented Tony, who always seemed to be eager to eat.

"Marti, I have some news," whispered Becky as she beckoned me aside. "What?"

"We're expecting a baby," she confided, "but don't tell anyone since I'm not more than a few weeks along."

"I think that's great! Now maybe you'll have that boy you want."

"Yeah, maybe, but I'm getting prepared for another girl."

"What are you going to do about doctors?" I asked.

"I'm going to keep the same one I have now and just come back to Statesville to have the baby," she replied.

"That's a lot of traveling, but I guess it's hard to change horses in midstream. Look, they're motioning for everyone to sit down. I'll see you after the banquet. Maybe we can all get together and celebrate!"

The meal was served and soon it was time for the speeches and awards presentation. As one of the linemen received his trophy, he spoke to the gathering.

"I'd just like to say thank you, and that I feel I wouldn't have received this honor if it hadn't been for the help Coach Carelli gave me. I honestly feel he's the best line coach I ever had." With that statement, he sat down.

I felt very proud that one of Al's players thought so highly of him. Coincidentally, both this boy and my husband would be going to the University of North Carolina the following year—the former to play football and the latter to teach, or, if there was any way possible, to coach football.

It was soon time for the head coach, Gene Abercrombie, to speak. He closed the festivities by saying that he regretted losing his two coaches, and that they had contributed greatly to the school's undefeated season. Then, clear out of the blue, he said, "But I guess Coach McClamrock will have enough to keep him busy, since he's expecting an addition to his family shortly." As everyone chuckled, I laughingly looked toward Becky and thought that she had told one too many about her secret.

It was late after the banquet, so we went straight home. Before going to bed we reminisced about our past two years in Statesville. It would be sad to leave, but the adventures of the future were ahead of us. We could hardly wait to experience the dawning of new days.

CHAPTER SEVENTEEN

June, 1968

"Please, please be careful with that dresser!" I shouted in anguish as Al and his two high school students began carrying the heavy, seventy-two-inch Italian Provincial dresser up the narrow cement stairway. As they rounded the tiny passageway into our upstairs apartment, one of the dresser's legs knocked against the wall. "Yipes! Can't you guys go a little slower?"

Actually, I should have been thankful that we had made it from Statesville to Chapel Hill without any catastrophes. Al had borrowed an open truck to haul our furniture in, and we had left Statesville at the crack of dawn. We had been working like the devil for the past two hours unloading items from the truck. I thought it odd that not one neighbor had offered to help us carry things into the apartment. Occasionally, I saw a face peering from one of the other apartment windows, but that was the extent of our welcome. I was beginning to wonder how I would like living in such a friendly neighborhood!

"Well, that was the last piece of furniture!" Al said, falling into the nearest chair. I saw a cloud of dust rise around him and realized how dirty everything must be. "I think we'll rest for half an hour before making the trip back. Will you and Vince be okay until I return?"

"Are you kidding? I'll have enough work here to keep me busy all night. When do you suppose you'll be getting back?" I asked noticing that it was four p.m.

"Probably not until two in the morning or later."

"If you're too tired to come back tonight, I want you to stay there and rest up. We'll be fine until you arrive, and I'd feel a lot better knowing you were getting a good night's sleep." I pulled up a box to sit on.

"We'll see, but as it stands now, I'll be on my way back this evening."

It was not long before Vince and I were left alone in the apartment to survey the mass confusion. The place seemed very cozy and compact. There were two bedrooms, one bathroom, a combined living and dining area and an extra-small kitchen. There were also wall-to-wall closets, a luxury we had not had in our rented home.

It seemed that everything was so close, especially after living in such a spacious home, but it gave me a warm sense of security rather than a closed-in effect. I liked it, and hurriedly began to put the furniture in its place. It was fun bathing Vince and putting him to bed in his new room. I worked for hours until I realized that I had had nothing to eat. I was beginning to wonder how I would survive without food when there was a knock on the door.

"Hi! We're your across-the-hall neighbors, John and Scotti Dupree," they greeted me cheerfully. I answered rather hesitantly, for I wondered where our cheerful neighbors had been this afternoon when we could have used a little help.

"Hi. I'm Marti Carelli, and my husband, Al, should be on his way back from Statesville sometime soon," I responded.

"We're just going to have a pizza. Care to come over and join us?"

"No, thank you. I really better stay here and wait for Al to get back," I answered, while hunger pangs stabbed through my stomach.

"Okay, but if you get hungry, come on over," they said and went into their apartment. They left their door open, and since our back door was open also, I heard their murmuring voices amidst a laugh or two. Suddenly, I was lonely and worried about Al. It was slightly after midnight and I knew from past experience that I would worry about him until he returned safely.

With the lights dimmed, I sat down in Al's easy chair and surveyed the apartment. Everything was in its place and the weariness of the day's events hit me. It had been gratifying work but it was finished; there was nothing left undone. Yet I needed to keep busy to keep from worrying. Deciding to pay our new neighbors a midnight visit, I stepped out into the hall and knocked on the open door.

"Come on in!" came a man's voice.

"It's just me—Marti," I answered weakly from the doorway. "I've changed my mind about the pizza offer."

"You just got here in time, then." I looked at the table and saw to my relief that there were still two pieces of pizza in the box.

"Here, you can have them both. John and I have had our fill," said Scotti as she pushed the box in my direction.

"Thanks. I guess I was hungrier than I thought." I began to eat.

"Well, we were, too. We just returned from Michigan, been driving all day and part of the night," replied John. I really felt guilty after I had secretly pre-condemned them for not offering to help us this afternoon. Between bites I said, "I was trying to guess all day who lived across the hall from us. Do you, by any chance, have any children?"

"One, a boy, Peter. He'll be a year old in January," said Scotti.

"Hey, that's great! I have a boy, Vince, who will be a year old in November. I was hoping there'd be children around for him to play with."

"There are quite a few children living in this area. In fact, there's another child in this building, a girl, Tricia, who lives directly below you," said Scotti.

"Do you work?" I asked her.

"Not anymore. I was with the Social Welfare Department, but quit before Peter was born. Why, do you?" She began clearing off the table.

"Not for the summer, but I'll be teaching in the fall. Al is here to get his Master's and he'll be teaching some freshman physical education courses."

"I've finished my course work for my Ph.D. in journalism and have my dissertation to complete. Hopefully, we'll be leaving Chapel Hill this January or next summer," added John.

I looked at my watch, realizing I had imposed on them too long. "Well, it's after one. I'd better let ya'll get some sleep. Thanks for everything."

"It was our pleasure," John answered. "We'll be anxious to meet your husband, so drop by sometime tomorrow."

"We sure will. Good night." I went across the hall back into our apartment. Al had still not returned by the time I finished my bath, so I crawled into bed. The last thing I remembered was hoping he had spent the night in Statesville and that nothing had happened to him on the way back to Chapel Hill. We had no telephone yet, so he couldn't call to let me know.

Vince woke me bright and early the next morning. Al still wasn't back, so I busied myself with small odd jobs. Around eleven-thirty he walked into the apartment. The moment I saw him, all the tension of the past hours vanished.

"You look refreshed," I murmured as we hugged each other.

"I hoped you wouldn't worry, but I did stay with Coach Ab last night. I was just too exhausted to drive back."

"I'm just happy you're here," I said, turning in time to see Vince crawling for the staircase. "No! No!" I ran to retrieve him before he fell down the steps. "We're really going to have to watch ourselves with this door. One careless time, and he'll find himself at the bottom of those horrible steps!"

Al took his son from my arms and began swinging him up and down. The rougher he was, the more Vince laughed. Contentedly, I watched them playing together as I cleared up the baby food jars and dishes. Al was home and the first day of our adventure had begun.

CHAPTER EIGHTEEN

September, 1968

As I walked up the incline toward the stadium, the gentle breeze blew against my face and the smell of fall was in the air. It was the exciting smell of football season. A low roar could be heard in the distance, reminding me of the sound of waves crashing against the beach on a still night. Fifty thousand voices were all cheering at once, an indication that the teams had entered the field for warm-ups.

I wound my way up the ramp to the second flight of seats and followed the numbers until I came to mine. It had a back to it and I was thankful, for once, that I could watch a football game in some semblance of comfort. With eyes squinted, I searched the sidelines for Al, but couldn't locate him. Even with my contact lenses, it was hard to see clearly at long distances—I realized why people brought binoculars to football games.

The teams left the field for the last preparations before the game started. Looking around, I saw that not one seat was empty. UNC was playing NC State, a big rival only twenty-nine miles away, and the number of fans for both teams was evenly distributed. I settled back, took a deep breath and tried to unwind. No matter what position Al had, whether it was player or coach, I was always keyed up for the game and couldn't relax until the finish, win or lose. As the band came onto the field to play the national anthem, I recalled the day in early June when Al's career had taken this new turn.

****

It was early afternoon. Vince and I were in front of the apartment building with Scotti and Peter. Both boys were crawling around in the grass, enjoying the soft blades that tickled their feet and legs.

"It's such a beautiful day," I sighed, stretching my tan legs out in front of me. "I could really get used to this life of daily cleaning, playing with Vince and relaxing!"

"I agree. It's nice, and I've waited for it long enough," replied Scotti.

"I know, and now it's my turn to work and wait for the days when I'll be a full-time housewife!" I jumped up to retrieve a pebble Vince had put into his mouth. "I'll tell you what really bugs me—hanging out the wash every day! Knowing we have a dryer we can't use here because there's no space makes it even worse."

"You'll get used to it," she calmly replied. "Guess I'll go in and put Peter down for his nap."

"I think I'll stay out here and wait for Al to get back from his class. He should be along any minute." I gave Vince some new toys to hold his attention while Scotti lugged Peter into the apartment building.

"Look what Mommy has," I said to Vince. I held a toy out in front of me and he crawled over to get it. As I watched his dexterity, I knew he would be walking in a matter of months.

Rumpling Vince's unmanageable hair, I thought of Al and his disillusionment over his teaching job at the university. Several days earlier, he had confided to me how he felt about it. We had just finished supper and Vince had been put to bed early. We cuddled together on the couch and a warm breeze filtered in through the open living room windows.

"You know, Marti, every day on my way to classes I have to pass the stadium and football offices and it's just tearing me apart," he moaned, his left hand brushing through his long hair, springing back the cowlick he had been trying to train for the past few weeks. "I want to coach football so badly I can taste it!"

"You will again," I tried to reassure him. "Who knows, you may even like teaching here so well that you'll want to go on and work for your Ph.D. in education. You could even wind up the head of a department in some major university."

"That may be true, but right this minute, I want to coach. I've even thought of stopping by Coach Dooley's office to offer to coach without pay, just to be coaching again," he admitted.

"Would we have enough money from my salary to live on and put you through school, if you gave up your assistantship?"

"I don't think so," he answered. "It's only a dream anyway."

That was the first and last time the subject was mentioned, but I had been concerned for Al. I wanted this next year to be a good one, and for that to happen, he had to be happy.

It was getting late, so I began gathering the toys together. I was stooping down to pick up Vince when I thought I heard my name being called from a distance. Looking up, I saw Al three blocks away. He looked as if he was running, yet his arms were swinging wildly above his head, and his feet were doing little dancing steps. As he approached, I heard him repeating my name as if to get my attention. He was running, and I was concerned until I noticed his extremely wide grin. His antics then seemed rather humorous. I was laughing at him when he finally reached us.

"Marti! Marti! I can't believe it! I really got it!" he stuttered, gasping for air.

"Slow down!" I commanded. "Did you run the whole way back?"

"I got it! I got it!" he yelled, picking me up and swinging me around. I had never seen him so excited—but I knew I wouldn't have an inkling about what was going on if he didn't calm down and stop jabbering.

"Calm yourself!" I laughed, as he dropped me to my feet. "Tell me what's happened and start from the beginning."

"All right. You remember how I said that I always go by the coaches' offices and how I was tempted to stop by and offer my services?"

"Yes."

"Well, on my way home, I did it! I stopped. Coach Dooley called me into his office and asked me about my coaching experience with the T formation. I had to admit that all I'd ever worked with was the Single Wing, but said I was determined to learn whatever was necessary."

"What did he say to that?" I asked hesitantly.

"He told me he was glad I'd leveled with him, and then we talked about his program. When he pulled out the pile of applications he'd received asking for graduate assistantships in coaching, I nearly fell over—there were quite a few."

"Al! Are you trying to tell me you got one?" My heart began to beat faster.

"Let me finish," he requested, moving over to sit down on the porch steps.

"Coach Dooley went on to explain that he liked the idea of my having coached before and he felt as if I would be willing to learn, which was important to him. It seems today one of his assistants decided to take a coaching job somewhere and he had a vacancy! He said that if I wanted to work hard, the job was mine!"

"Yeah!" I shouted, jumping up and dancing around. Excitedly, we ran into the apartment building to share the good news with our new closest friends, the Duprees.

****

The cheering of the crowds brought my attention back to the field where the players, followed by the coaches, were running down the sidelines. I spotted Al by the way that he limped when he ran, something he had done since his knee operation. It was slight but noticeable to me. My attention remained on him most of the game and I was happy when we came out the winners.

I shuffled out of the stadium and went to the field house to wait for him. When I arrived, I noticed that most of the other coaches' wives were already there mingling among the crowd of well-wishers. I went up to Jane, one of the few that I had met.

"Hi, Marti," she cheerily greeted me. "Where were you sitting?"

"Somewhere near the thirty-five yard line. I had to sit alone this time," I responded and looked toward the door, hoping Al would soon appear.

"Next game, remind me, and I'll give you one of my extra tickets so you can sit with the rest of the wives," she said, nodding to one of the players who had just returned from the dressing room.

"That would be nice of you. It's much better to watch the game with someone."

"Here comes Moe. Excuse me. I'll probably see you later," she exclaimed as she ran to meet her husband.

Al was one of the last to emerge from the field house, but I was so pleased to see him that the past hour of waiting meant nothing.

"Hi," he said as he reached for my hand and gave it a squeeze. I knew from the look on his face that he was pleased and happy. In that instant, I realized that no matter what degrees he earned, coaching would always be his life's work.

CHAPTER NINETEEN

October, 1968

"Are your Danish rolls finished yet?" I hollered across the hall to Scotti as I finished setting the table for breakfast.

"Give me about five more minutes," came her response.

It was rather unusual for two families to hit it off as well as we did and it made living in a small apartment much more pleasant. Usually, the doors between the apartments were left open, and since we had fenced off part of the hallway as a play area for the boys, it seemed more like one large apartment rather than two small ones.

It was the end of the month of October and both families were still two days away from payday. Each of us was out of money and just about out of food, so as we had done in the past, we were pooling our resources in order to have a well-balanced breakfast.

"At last! The bacon is fried and the pancakes are ready," I called to Al and John, who were patiently waiting to eat.

"What a shame to make you work so hard on your twenty-fifth birthday," teased John, throwing down the newspaper and going out into the hall to close the door to his apartment. "That ought to keep Vince and Peter from wandering where they ought not be." He picked Peter up and placed him on the rug in the middle of the living room.

"Here they are," Scotti exclaimed, putting the hot rolls on the table. "Oh, we can't begin without the syrup. I'll be back in a sec!" She rushed over to her kitchen.

"Are you gals finally ready?" asked Al as we prepared to sit down.

"Let's eat," I said, finding a place for the butter on our overcrowded table. "I hope you guys are prepared to clean up this mess."

"Now, wait a minute!" interjected Al. "No one said anything about our doing the dishes."

"It's only fair," Scotti said.

"We'll talk about it later. Let's eat." John helped himself to a pile of pancakes.

"By the way, have you started writing your dissertation yet?" I asked John.

"No, but the research is completed. It looks like we won't be leaving here until this coming June."

"If we don't go then, they'll probably kick us out!" put in Scotti.

"Well, I'm glad you're not leaving earlier. The way it looks now, Al may be here until the end of next year's football season and I don't relish the idea of breaking in new neighbors. We couldn't be this lucky again." I polished off my last piece of bacon.

"Well, John, we'll treat you to a lavish dinner at The Barn when it comes time to celebrate the end of your toils," offered Al.

"Yeah! I love that place. I can't wait until we have something to celebrate so we can go there." I lit a cigarette.

"Speaking of celebrations, aren't you in for one tonight?" asked Scotti as she poured the coffee.

"Thanks to Al's parents, we have some birthday money. He's taking me to the Ranch House this evening for dinner," I proudly announced. "It kind of makes me feel guilty knowing you'll be home eating hot dogs or something." They laughed.

"Let's get the dishes finished," Al said, dragging himself out of his chair into the kitchen.

"Let's leave before they change their minds!" Scotti suggested. We took our coffee and cigarettes and retired to her apartment.

That night, Al and I had a lovely quiet dinner and returned to the apartment. As we came to the top of the stairs, Al suggested we stop by for a short visit with the Duprees. When the door opened, I was stunned by a cry of "Surprise!" The two other families from the apartment building were there and a cake with twenty-five candles was sitting on the table. All in all, my birthday was a beautiful day spent with wonderful friends and I was thankful.

Several months later, in the early spring, we were able to celebrate John's accomplishments in obtaining his Ph.D. in journalism. We went to The Barn and toasted our friendship, realizing that in a month or so we would be going our separate ways. The Duprees would head for New Mexico in June. In January, Al would get his degree and we would be looking for a new job and home. Knowing that we would probably see little of each other over the years made the celebration bittersweet.

The Duprees moved in June with Scotti expecting another baby the next fall. The apartment building seemed empty and the summer days passed slowly. However, fall soon was upon us. The excitement of football season, combined with the knowledge that Al would soon complete his studies, gave us much to look forward to.

CHAPTER TWENTY

November, 1969

One of my students stuck her head around my half-open office door. "Mrs. Carelli, the girls are dressed and ready for exercises."

"I'll be out in a minute. Tell the girls to line up in the gym," I answered as I squashed my cigarette out in the overflowing ashtray.

I was grateful to have acquired a teaching position in a school much closer to Chapel Hill, but just could not seem to get with it. The students didn't respond as in years past, which I attributed to the fact that I was dissatisfied. My home and family were more important to me than teaching, and I was continually worrying about what I should be doing at home.

I looked at my large wall calendar and its rows of crossed-off dates. Every day that I marked another "x" in a square made me more certain that I was pregnant. Before coming to school that morning, I had dropped off a urine specimen at the doctor's office for a pregnancy test. I'd been putting off calling for test results, afraid they might be negative. This was my last class for the day and the call could only be postponed one more hour. Taking a deep breath in preparation for the sixth-period noise and confusion, I left the office and took the basement steps two at a time. The hour dragged by.

"Okay, class dismissed. You have seven and a half minutes to dress, so let's hit it!" I directed the students as they rushed for the locker room and their showers. "Sue, if anyone needs me, I'll be in the office. Take my book and whistle and be in charge until I return," I told one of my more dependable students, and pushed through the swinging doors into the hall.

When I came to the main office to telephone, I was relieved to see that it was empty. I was nervous enough without having the principal overhear my conversation. With little regret, I remembered I had told him that I planned on teaching at this school for at least two years. I picked up the phone, trembling so much that I had to redial the number.

"Hello," came the stilted voice of the nurse.

"Hi. This is Mrs. Carelli and I'm calling in regard to my pregnancy test. Do you have the results ready?" I asked, while my hands began to sweat and my stomach fluttered.

"One moment, please, while I check." It seemed as if she was gone for several minutes rather than a few seconds. "Yes, we have those results. They were negative, Mrs. Carelli." I just couldn't believe it. I was so positive that I was pregnant.

"Are you sure?" I stammered.

"We're as sure as we can be this early," she answered. "If you still think you're pregnant in a week, try the test again. About ten percent of the time we're wrong, but in that case it's usually a false positive."

"All right, but first I'd like to ask a question. The directions I was given about the test were that I wasn't to drink anything after ten o'clock up until my first morning specimen. If I had eaten jello, would that have interfered with the test?"

"Jello is made out of water, Mrs. Carelli, and could very well contribute to a negative result when a positive one was in order," she reproved.

"All right. Thank you. I'll have another test run in a week if my period hasn't started." Despondently, I hung up the phone. "Darn! Why couldn't I have had more control?" I muttered to myself, remembering the jello I had eaten the night before. I really hadn't thought it would hurt, and naturally the minute I knew I couldn't have any water was the minute I got thirsty!

I returned to the locker room, locked the doors and left, picking up Vince at the babysitter's on the way home. I knew Al would be anxious to hear the test results too.

Once we got home, Vince clamored for my attention. "Mommy, look what I did," he said proudly, handing me a piece of paper with a lot of scribbly red marks all over it.

"Why, that's very pretty," I said, and gave him a squeeze.

"It's a house." I was relieved he'd told me that before I said they were nice red worms!

"When are we going to eat?" he asked. Once again, I marveled at how grown up he acted for a two-year-old.

"In a minute. Why don't you go play in your room with your toy cars while I fix supper? Daddy will be home soon."

"Okay," and off he ran. I heard the toys clattering around as I prepared a fast casserole and set the table.

"Hi." Al came into the kitchen laden with books.

"Did you get much work done on your paper today?" I inquired, placing the napkins under the forks.

"Just about finished. What did the doctor say?"

"The test was negative," I answered. "But I believe it was only because I ate jello last night."

"What does that have to do with a pregnancy test?"

"I wasn't supposed to have water and I didn't really think about jello actually being water, so the test could have been inaccurate. Anyway, I'm supposed to have another one done in a week."

"Then it'll cost you twice as much," Al reminded me. "Why don't you make an appointment with our family doctor to have that black mole taken off your foot? You can ask him to do the test while you're there." He called Vince to the table.

I did call and make an appointment for later that week. Al picked up Vince from the sitter's and the two of them met me in the doctor's office after school.

"Gee, Al, I'm so shaky. I don't know if I want to hear what the results are, just in case I'm not really pregnant," I said, sitting down on a brown, faded sofa to wait my turn. "I want to be pregnant so badly that I'm afraid I might have one of those false pregnancies where you actually get big and can even go through labor, yet have no baby."

"Honey, just calm down. It won't be the end of the world if you're not pregnant. We have a lot of time to keep trying." He patted my folded hands.

"I know, but Vince will already be almost three when this baby is born, if there is a baby in there," I said as I pressed my hands to my flat stomach. "Besides, it would be a perfect way to get out of my teaching contract. I'd rather say I'm pregnant than say my husband is getting a new job, especially since they asked me how long you'd be here."

"We'll know in a little while," he reassured me. Then the nurse called my name, and I went back into the inner office to wait for the doctor.

"What's your trouble?" he asked, rushing into the room. I wondered how doctors ever kept from having ulcers, because they always seemed to be in such a hurry.

"It's my right foot. There's a suspicious-looking mole on top of it, and I haven't had my period for almost two months."

"That's quite a combination of problems," he chuckled. "Give the nurse a urine sample, and while she's checking that out, we'll take off this mole." He directed me to the bathroom.

When I returned, he removed the mole while I tried to think of something else. It didn't hurt, but the way I was feeling, almost anything could make me sick.

"That's taken care of," he said, putting the remains on a tray. "We'll send it to the lab, and if for any reason it comes out malignant, we'll give you a call."

"Great!" I thought. "If I have cancer, they'll call me!"

"Now," the doctor continued, "I'll go see about your specimen and be back with you in a moment." He was only gone a minute or two when, once more, he rushed into the room. "Looks like you're going to be a mother," he said, surveying me for some kind of reaction. His face lit up the minute I cried, "I'm so happy!"

When I went back out to the waiting room to meet Al, he could tell by my face that the news was good. He and I walked Vince across the street to a chicken place to have dinner and celebrate. Once we were seated at our table, I turned to Vince and said, "Guess what?"

"What?" he asked eagerly, thinking we were going to play our guessing game.

"Next summer, in July sometime, you're going to have a new baby brother or sister. Would you like that?"

He thought seriously for a moment, then answered, "Not if it's a girl. I want a brother."

"Vince, we can't be sure which it will be, but if it's a girl, you should be happy too," Al reproved gently.

"I don't know. I'm hungry," our outspoken child said, dipping a french fry into a puddle of ketchup.

"Just think. This time next year, we'll be four instead of three! I wonder where we'll be living by that time—and where our second baby will be born." I smiled into Al's deep brown eyes, which were narrowed reflectively. I could tell that he too was wondering what the future held for us.

CHAPTER TWENTY-ONE

January, 1970

"Hello," I said into the telephone receiver.

"Hi, hon, how are you doing without me?" Al asked. He was in Washington, D.C., for the annual football coaches' convention. Each evening he called to fill me in on the details of his day. He had traveled to the convention as part of the UNC staff and was hoping to find a new coaching position in a university before returning.

"It's a real struggle, but I'm managing," I joked. "Anything new turn up today?"

"No offers, if that's what you mean. The East Carolina coach did hint about an upcoming position, if I was willing to wait until June. Naturally, I told him I needed a job now and couldn't wait that long."

"That's the truth! Anything else?"

"I've met a lot of coaches who are looking around to fill positions on their staffs. I've even had several interviews. So far, most of them have said they were impressed with me, but they're looking for someone with a little more age and experience. I do have one possibility—I ran into a guy I knew from my high school coaching days, and he told me he'd been offered the position of line coach at Marshall University, but had to turn it down because of his commitments to the high school where he's coaching now. He gave me the head coach's name and told me he'd see him tomorrow and put in a good word for me."

"Marshall University?" I asked. "I've never heard of it. Where is it?"

"It's one of the two state schools of West Virginia and it's located in Huntington, one of the state's largest cities," he answered.

"Do you think you have a chance of getting the job?"

"There's always a chance, Marti. What impressed me was that the head coach, Rick Tolley, is young and so is his staff."

"Well, do you have an interview with him?"

"No, but I'll work on that tomorrow. I've got to go to some cocktail party now, so don't forget that I love you, and I'll try to call tomorrow evening at about the same time. Give Vince a kiss for me and tell him I'll bring him back a surprise."

"All right. I miss you! Think about me," I said, hanging up the phone. We had both been really counting on this convention to produce a job for Al. It was the first part of January and my resignation had been accepted as of the first of February. That meant that, unless Al was earning money by then, we would have no income. We were both excited at the prospect of moving, but the tension of job-hunting in a field that was already overcrowded made us irritable. "There are still two more days before this convention is over, and no one knows what tomorrow will bring," I said encouragingly to myself. Dismissing the subject from my mind, I went to bed.

The next day passed as the previous four had, slowly and drearily. I thought constantly about Al and what he was probably doing at certain times of the day. When the phone rang that evening, I rushed to it eagerly, knowing it was him.

"Hi, Al," I said into the receiver.

"How did you know it was me?" he asked.

"I don't know, I just did. I'm afraid to ask. Did you see or speak with Coach Tolley?"

"Sure did, and was definitely impressed. Right now, it looks like we just might be moving to West Virginia," he said with hidden excitement in his voice.

"Oh, really!" I exclaimed, feeling a twinge of excitement myself.

"He's the first coach to approach me with a solid offer. He knows what he's looking for and he's told me that I fit the bill, if I want the job!"

"What did you tell him?" I asked with bated breath.

"I told him I was honestly interested in the position, but that I wanted to see the campus, town and whole set-up before I made a definite decision."

"Did he agree to it?"

"Uh-huh. Soon after I come home tomorrow, I'll be flying to Huntington to look the situation over."

"Gee, I hope it's a nice place. How long will you get to be home before you take off again?" I asked.

"A couple of days. It'll take time for Rick to work out the details of my arrival."

"I am so relieved. A real offer—I can't believe it!" I said, feeling the pressures of the past months slowly ease from my body.

"Good night, honey. I'll see you tomorrow afternoon. Don't forget that I love you," he said.

"Night, love," I answered and hung up the telephone. Sleep was impossible, so I ran downstairs to talk to our neighbors, the Russells. We had become good friends in the past few months, and I had to tell someone the news!

Several days after Al's return, he once again made preparations for a trip—this time to Huntington.

"Don't forget to call tonight," I reminded him. "Remember I'll be waiting to hear from you, so don't keep me in suspense for too long."

"I won't. I know you have as much at stake as I do and you'll hear from me as soon as it's feasible to call," he promised. Giving Vince and me a hug, he left for the airport. When the car was out of sight, Vince and I took a long walk and later treated ourselves to sandwiches at a local hamburger place. Al's call came about ten-thirty that evening.

"I've accepted the job. I am the new offensive line coach for Marshall University's football team!" he reported proudly.

"I'm so pleased! Tell me what the place is like."

For the next half-hour, Al told me about the town. It was an industrial place with many houses built closely together because of the hilly terrain. The university was unlike UNC in that it was located in the center of town, crowded together in an area the size of several city blocks. To appreciate it, you needed to walk on the part of the campus that wasn't visible from the city's busy streets. They were in the process of constructing new buildings and a new football stadium, with a field that would be covered in Astroturf. Housing would be a problem and we had to be prepared to pay higher rent.

"Will you have any time to look for a house while you're there?" I asked after his last remark.

"No. I'm coming home tomorrow morning and will have a week to set up a moving date for you and Vince. It looks like I'll be coming back here to work and live until I find a suitable home for all of us."

"How long do you estimate that Vince and I will be here without you?" I asked, not liking that part of it.

"I can't say. Maybe until the first of February or shortly after," he answered.

"Golly, that means three weeks or more!" The more I heard about this arrangement, the less I liked it.

"Let's discuss all this when I come home," he said, closing the subject.

"Okay. We'll see you soon. Bye." I sat at the desk near the phone for several minutes, trying to let everything that had been said sink in. I was relieved and happy that Al had finally begun the career he loved so much. "Marshall University, here we come!" I said to myself, finding it hard to believe our good fortune.

CHAPTER TWENTY-TWO

February, 1970

"Run like this!" Al said to Vince as he demonstrated the swinging arm and leg motions.

"Okay!" he answered enthusiastically, and began running after his father down the slope of the road. I snapped another picture, advancing the film as I began walking faster to catch up with them.

Unable to catch them, I shouted, "Wait for your old pregnant mother!"

"Whoa!" Al said, pretending to put on his invisible brakes. "You tired yet?" he asked Vince.

"Yes," he answered. Al hoisted him to his shoulders and we began walking once more.

The walk was our farewell hike around Chapel Hill. Al was leaving in the morning and would not return. The movers were planning to come around the thirteenth of February, and we wouldn't all meet again until Vince and I flew into Huntington on the fifteenth.

As we passed the construction area where the old student housing buildings were being torn down to make room for new hospital additions, Al commented, "We sure had a good year and a half here."

"In a way, I'll miss it," I answered. "I guess all along I was really hoping a position would open up for you here so we could make this our home."

"It's like Coach Dooley said—the offer I have is more than he can make me at this time. It doesn't necessarily mean we won't be coming back. He left me with the impression that, if ever anything opened up, I'd be one of the first he would consider for the job. I hate leaving here too, but I'll have more coaching responsibilities at Marshall than I could have had here because the staff there is smaller," he said.

"I know you're right. It's just that I've enjoyed the wives of the coaches here and now I'm going to have to begin meeting people all over again."

"That part of it shouldn't bother you—it'll be fine. Are you ready to go in yet? It looks like our 'young-un' has fallen asleep." He readjusted Vince's small body in his arms.

"I'm tired, too. I'm gaining too much weight too fast." I looked down at the maternity clothes I was already wearing. "I can't believe I'm so fat so soon!"

"It must be psychological," Al said. "The minute you realized you were pregnant, you knew you didn't have to hold your stomach in any longer, so you've been letting it all hang out. Now it's too late to get that control back, so you're fat!" He laughed.

"Thanks a lot," I answered, holding the door of the apartment open for the two of them to pass through.

"Don't you feel just a little sad?" I asked him.

"Yes, I do," he confessed, laying Vince on his bed and heading into our bedroom to pack his clothes.

There was so much to do that the next few weeks slid by. Al called frequently to tell me about the houses he had found. It was difficult for him to really communicate what they looked like; his descriptions always seemed a little less than bright. So far, we had been unable to agree on anything he had found, and time was fast becoming our enemy—we had only one more week to find a suitable home.

I could tell that house-hunting was getting him down, because it meant he was unable to devote his entire energies to his job and he always hated to do anything halfway. Three nights before the movers were scheduled to arrive, I decided that I would agree to whatever new house he had found that day, regardless of what it looked like. His call came later than usual.

"You won't believe this, but I've found us a house that I believe you'll really like," he said exhaustedly. "I'm calling so late because I've just come from the place."

"That's a relief!" I whispered, almost afraid to hear about it.

"I had just been driving around, really depressed over the whole affair, when the realtor I was with begged me to make one more stop to see a house he had heard was for rent. It hadn't been advertised so he didn't know much about it. The husband of the woman who cares for the place was there and willingly showed us around. Marti, it has a huge backyard for Vince to play in and it's located in a nice area."

"How many bedrooms does it have?" I interrupted.

"Let's see. It has three bedrooms, one bathroom, a nice-size living room, a kitchen with plenty of cabinet space, and a small area that could be used for a utility room," he finished.

"What about a dining room?"

"It's the only thing I could think of that you wouldn't like about the house, but we can put our dining room table and chairs comfortably into the kitchen."

"That must mean there's no dining room," I said dryly, trying to remember the promise I had made to myself earlier that day.

"Correct." I could tell he was waiting to hear some argument.

"Can we rent it?" I asked, not really trusting Al's judgment about this house, but willing to sacrifice my own concerns just to have a place to move into.

"That's why I called so late. Mr. Watkeys, the man who showed us around, told me that his wife had complete control of the house, including who would be renting it. Since she wasn't home, I had to wait to hear from her. She just hung up before I called you."

"Were we able to rent it?" I asked impatiently.

"She said it had always been her policy to interview the couples who wanted to rent it, but since you weren't here, she was willing to go on what her husband had said about me, and she felt certain that we would be desirable tenants."

After Al gave me the new address, we hung up. I had sensed his relief and made a pledge to myself that I wouldn't show disappointment in the house—no matter what it looked like.

The next three days were busy ones. I had to do a lot of the packing and all of the directing—telling the movers what to do. The Russells downstairs were very helpful, watching Vince and feeding us most of our meals.

My last night in the apartment was a lonely one, and since Al and I would be spending Valentine's Day apart, I consoled myself by composing a simple poem for him. Sitting at the little Early American maple desk that he had bought when we first moved to Chapel Hill, I wrote.

February 14, 1970

YOU AND A DAY

In the morning upon awaking,
I reach outward for the safety of your warmth and—nestle.
Comforted, it enfolds me in a genial embrace
Thus, my first thoughts of this new day focus on YOU.

The morning passes in play with our son—so young, so
*   innocent, so loving*
Yet while we idle away the morning moments
Enjoying the outside world that God has given us,
There are mixtures of thoughts of just YOU—Daddy.

Naps and mundane tasks occupy the afternoon,
All is tranquil, unreal—when
"Mommy! Daddy! Morning!" obliterates the calm.
Once again, our thoughts turn to YOU—Daddy.

While I am busy in the kitchen laughter can be heard,
Father and son are romping in the love of each other's company.
Supper is ready and getting cold
Suddenly quiet descends and YOU—Daddy are leading the prayer.

As we hear those childish words, "More juice, Mommy,"
Bedtime has come with all its frustrating glory.
With a kiss and a hug for each of us,
Our son wants his Daddy for that all-important
one last hug and kiss goodnight.

As the night creeps onward, we find ourselves weary and climb into bed,
A few last thoughts expressed—we cling to one another
A goodnight kiss, a whisper of love, a sleepy sigh,
Turning, I gently reach toward the peace slowly engulfing my mind
filled with its last thoughts of YOU.

I placed the pen back into its holder and the poem in an envelope. After sealing and addressing it, I walked to the corner mailbox. I knew we would be together before my poem reached Al, but the lonely ache had vanished, leaving in its place an overwhelming love for my little family.

Early the next morning, the movers arrived and hurriedly packed their van, promising to see me again in a few days. Just before the Russells took Vince and me to the airport, Al called.

"Everything settled?" he asked.

"Yes," I answered, anxious to be on my way. "The movers have left and will be in Huntington in three days."

"All right, then. I'll see you tonight." As an afterthought, he added, "Don't be frightened when you land at the Huntington airport. It's scary and gives you the sensation that the plane will run right off the runway over the mountain."

"Okay. See you soon!" I said, not giving much thought to an airport that was located on the top of some mountain.

CHAPTER TWENTY-THREE

February, 1970

"I'll help you with that," said a handsome, elderly man as he took my traveling case from me. "It looks like you have your hands full."

"Thank you. I'd appreciate it," I answered, shifting Vince's dead weight from my right side to my left.

"Will someone be picking you up?"

"Oh, yes. My husband will be here for us. We've just moved to Huntington." One of the airport officials took Vince from my arms and carried him down the ramp. When we reached the gate, he had awakened and the man set him down. Taking my son's hand, I hurriedly headed for the shelter of the lounge—I had been unprepared for the biting cold that ripped through my thin coat.

In my rush to find Al, I forgot the benefactor who was dutifully lugging my case.

"Madame, where would you like me to set this?" he asked kindly.

"Oh! Right here is fine," I answered, indicating the closest row of seats. "I guess my husband is late, because I don't see him." In fact, the place was practically deserted.

"Would you like me to wait with you?" he asked.

"No, thank you. I'll be fine. I'm sure he'll be here shortly, and I don't mind waiting a few more minutes after the hours we spent in Richmond waiting for a flight out."

"All right, if you're sure." He tipped his hat in farewell.

Five minutes later, Al appeared, rushing through the lounge.

"I'm sorry I'm late, but I got lost," he said as he picked up Vince and gave me a hug.

"I didn't realize we'd get in so late. It's nearly 10:00 p.m." My legs were aching and I was ready for sleep.

"We'll get the luggage and go on over to the motel. I'd like you to see the house, too—it's only a few blocks from there."

It was the last thing I wanted to do, but rather than complain, I agreed. My first sight of the Huntington area was in the dead of night, and I could only feel the mountainous roads as we traveled toward our new home. As we came closer to our destination, the winds died down but the biting cold was still with us.

"Is it always this cold?" I asked as we pulled into the Stone Lodge Motel.

"We've had snow flurries at least once a day since I've been here," Al answered. I tried to calculate how long it would take me to adjust to this cold weather.

From the motel we went to the house. I could barely make out the styles of homes along the bumpy road, but I was aware of the closeness of everything.

"You were right about the houses being built close together, but you never mentioned the continuous potholes in the roads," I said as we pulled up before a small white house with a dark roof.

"It has something to do with the weather. Every spring they repair the roads, but by the end of the next winter they're just like they were before. A lot of the roads were brick at one time, and the paving was done over that," he explained and opened the car door. Mr. and Mrs. Watkeys greeted us in the driveway.

"I hope this isn't too inconvenient, but I wanted my wife to see the house and to meet you."

"No, it's quite all right," answered Mrs. Watkeys. Both she and her husband had graying hair and were of medium build. They explained that they had three children, some in our age range, and several grandchildren. It didn't take long before we both felt like we had known them all our lives, and I was relieved to know that they were so congenial. When Al had told me the landlord lived next door, I had imagined all sorts of potential problems.

As we entered the house, I was surprised at its pleasant layout.

"I really am pleased by all this cabinet space!" I said as my eyes traveled around the cozy kitchen and utility room. "After the tiny apartment kitchen I'm used to, this seems like a mansion."

"This is the back entrance," explained Mrs. Watkeys. "From this window, you can see the backyard, and it does extend quite far." I peered out the small window but was unable to see farther than the area lit by the small back porch light.

"This is the living room," she continued as I inspected the house, mentally placing our furniture here and there. It was all very adequate and I was glad I hadn't said anything about not believing Al could find a house that I would enjoy. I had grossly misjudged his ability to do so, and I privately reprimanded myself.

Making plans to return the next day, we exhaustedly returned to the motel and enjoyed a good night's sleep.

The following day was spent in last-minute cleaning and figuring out just where to put the furniture. We decided to spend the night at the house rather than the motel, since we expected the movers around six o'clock the next morning. The Watkeys generously supplied us with sleeping bags and blankets, and these we placed in the room we had chosen for the nursery.

Much to our surprise, we woke up the next morning to see a white blanket of snow outside the windows. The movers called and said they would still arrive that morning, but a little later than expected. We were hungry but didn't want to leave the house before the movers arrived. However, our hunger problem was solved when Mr. Watkeys came to our door with an invitation to a good West Virginia breakfast.

By mid-afternoon, the movers had come and gone. Everything was unpacked and strewn about the floor. As we had done in our previous moves, we worked most of the day and night until everything was in its place. In the wee hours of the morning, we were able to sit in our new living room, feeling the aches slowly creeping throughout our bodies, yet enjoying the sensations because the result of our hard work was so gratifying. Savoring, for a while, our ability to make a home comfortable, we headed for the bedroom.

The next morning, we went out for breakfast—one of my favorite treats. Then Al gave Vince and me a tour of the university and his new office.

"It's not nearly as bad as it looks from the outside," I commented to Al as the three of us sat down on a bench in the middle of the campus. "I guess I was comparing this to the open spaces we enjoyed at Lenoir Rhyne, but here, there are twenty times more students and every inch of space is needed. The more I see of it, the more I'm beginning to enjoy it."

"Let's go to the stadium," Al suggested.

"Give me your hand, Vince. We're going to see where the boys play football," I told him, seeing that the tour had tired him and his eyelids were drooping. By the time we arrived, he was sound asleep. Leaving our son in the car, Al led me to the fence surrounding the field.

The field was still under construction. In fact, it was in complete chaos, with bleachers torn apart, cement everywhere, and mud—lots of it! I tried to visualize what it would look like when it was completed, while Al pointed out what was being done.

They were hoping, he explained, that the turf and most of the bleachers would be ready for the first game, but the field house with its dressing rooms would not be complete for another year. That would complicate matters somewhat, since they would have to transport the boys to and from the physical education building in buses for each game, but Al said it would be worth the wait.

His words conjured up such a vivid picture that I soon saw what he did: the flags surrounding the stadium blowing in the breeze, the green and white bleachers, the brightness of the turf, the band in colorful uniforms, the majorettes and pom-pom girls in shorts and little skirts, and the boys in clean uniforms running across the field to the sounds of cheering fans. It seemed so real that he startled me when he spoke.

"Marti, I love it!" Al said fervently. Arm in arm we turned toward the car.

CHAPTER TWENTY-FOUR

July, 1970

"Happy birthday to you, happy birthday to you. Happy birthday, dear Pop-Pop, happy birthday to you!" Vince's childish voice could be heard above the flat singing of the adults.

"Blow out the candles and make a wish," I urged Dad Carelli as Vince leaned down to help him.

It was July eighteenth, Dad's fiftieth birthday. The Carellis had arrived several days before in hopes that the baby would be born on its scheduled date of July fifteenth, but we had no such luck. Mom Carelli planned to stay with Vince and Al while I was in the hospital, and would help out for a week after I returned home. Although he hadn't said anything, since the baby hadn't come on its due date, I knew Al had secretly hoped it would come on one of his parents' birthdays. If it didn't arrive today, we'd miss Dad's, but we still had Mom's to hope for in three days.

"Gosh, Dad, I'm sorry I haven't had this baby yet," I said as Mom cut a piece of cake for each of us. "How long will you be able to stay before you have to get back to New Jersey?"

"I won't have to leave until this weekend, since this is my vacation." Never before had the Carellis planned to stay with us so long—usually their visits were crammed into a short weekend. Al seemed very pleased that they didn't have to rush off this time.

"Marti, I'll do that," Mom commanded as I began clearing the table. "You should be off your feet, so go sit down!" She was right. This was a difficult pregnancy as far as my legs were concerned. A weight gain of forty pounds had contributed greatly to the condition of my varicose veins, and I regretted that I hadn't controlled my eating habits.

"I've got an idea." I propped my feet up on the nearest chair. "Today would be the perfect time for us to take Vince to Camden Park. Maybe all that walking will induce Junior to make his entrance into this world." We had been hoping for another boy for many reasons—partially because I had all male baby clothes!

"Suits me," everyone responded. So climbing into the air-conditioned car, we headed for the amusement park.

Later, as Al and I waited for Vince and his grandparents to return from their train ride, he said, grinning, "You are the most beautiful pregnant woman in the park."

"I don't know about being the prettiest one here," I retorted, surveying my fashionable maternity clothes, "but there's no doubt that I'm the largest!"

"Are you feeling all right?" he asked me as we walked toward one of the train station's benches.

"I'm having a great time, but I'm getting hungry. Really, though, I shouldn't eat another morsel of food until this baby is born!" I said.

"Mommy! Daddy! Did you see Pop-Pop, Grammy and me on the train?" Vince asked eagerly as Dad Carelli handed him to Al.

"We certainly did! Did you see anything interesting?" He proceeded to give us all the intricate details of his train ride. As we arrived at one of the cafes on the grounds, I dropped back and walked beside Mom. Dad and Al were walking ahead of us with Vince between them, each of them holding one of his little hands.

"That would make a beautiful picture!" I said to Mom, pulling out my camera. Watching the three of them walking together sent a wave of warmth through my body.

The park visit was a big success. When we arrived home, Vince was ready for a lengthy nap. Al, who liked to keep busy, suggested a trip to his office and he and Dad took off out the front door.

"You know, Mom, Al is very proud of his office. The day he took Vince and me there, he was bubbling over about it."

"Does he seem to be happy here?" she asked with motherly concern. "It's so far away from us."

"I doubt that he'll be here very long." The two of us went out into the coolness of the backyard, lemonade in hand. "As you know, he hated leaving Carolina, but he's very pleased about the additional responsibility he has here. He needs the experience before he can return to UNC for a similar position," I explained as we pulled the lawn chairs under the shade of a huge apple tree. "He plans to stay here for two years, unless something should break for him sooner."

"I hope I'm not sounding like a nosy mother-in-law. It's just that it's so far to come to see you."

"I'm getting rather used to this place, and that's something I thought I'd never say," I said, trying to shift my weight and get comfortable. "Damn! I wish this baby would come!"

Much to my disgust, the baby did not arrive on Mom Carelli's birthday or even before the weekend. Soon it was time for Dad to go back to work. Leaving Mom behind to wait with us, he prepared to leave.

"Do you have everything?" Mom questioned Dad. "You'll be all right now until I get home?"

"Sure I will," he answered, pulling her to him for a last embrace. Their parting reminded me of young lovers, filling me with gladness that I had been fortunate enough to become part of their family.

"You take care of the plane reservations and let me know if you need any money." He settled himself behind the wheel of their brown Cadillac.

"I believe Mom wishes she were leaving with you," I teased. Since Dad Carelli was driving their car back, Mom would fly home later—her first experience in an airplane. She was clearly not looking forward to the ordeal, but was trying to be brave.

"I'm not afraid," she reassured everyone. Al moved toward the car window and, with a handshake, his father bade him his last farewell.

CHAPTER TWENTY-FIVE

August 4, 1970

"She's going to call the doctor in a little while, but I'm beginning to worry about her," Mom Carelli said to Dad on the telephone. I was sitting on the front porch and overheard the tail end of their conversation. I appreciated her concern, but the only thing that worried Al or me was that this birth, like Vince's, might be a breech.

Tomorrow would make the baby three weeks overdue, and I had gained several more pounds just sitting around waiting for my first pain. My doctor was on vacation and I had made an appointment with his substitute out of sheer desperation. I had been so uncomfortable the past few weeks that I could hardly wait to feel the pain of an honest-to-goodness contraction.

Mom came out onto the porch. "What time do you leave?" she inquired gently, for my anxiety was evident.

"In a few minutes."

"Will you be able to drive the car all right?" Her eyes wandered to our small Volkswagon.

"Sure. I think I'll leave now." I was really anxious to find out if this doctor would be willing to put me in the hospital for inducement of labor. I was positive my original doctor would have been concerned enough by this time to have done it.

I was gone for several hours and when I returned, dinner was on the table. Al came to the door to greet me. "Any news?" he asked. His concern made me wonder if he and his mother had been discussing me while I was gone.

"I couldn't talk the doctor into putting me into the hospital, but he did give me some concoction to take. I believe part of it is castor oil. If I'm ready to deliver, this should make my contractions begin," I replied, collapsing on the sofa.

"Dinner is ready," he said, trying to comfort me.

"I'm sorry, but I don't want to eat. If I'm to go into labor, I want to make sure it's on an empty stomach." I stretched my cumbersome body the full length of the couch.

Later that evening, before going to bed, Mom Carelli tried to console me.

"When I delivered Linda, it took me twelve hours after I received the castor oil before labor began."

"In that case, I still have several more hours of hope," I said dryly.

"Just try to get some sleep," she said, leading me into the bedroom where Al had retired earlier. Mom looked extremely tired and I realized the past few weeks had taken their toll on everyone's nerves.

"I'm sorry I've been so moody," I apologized as she turned out the overhead light.

"At least try to rest," she whispered and softly closed the door.

Around midnight I was awakened by what seemed to be a contraction. However, it was so light that I thought at first I must be imagining things. When the second one occurred, I noted the time on a piece of paper that I had left on the nightstand. By two o'clock a.m., the pains were five minutes apart, but not much stronger. I woke Al.

"Honey, I think I'm in labor," I said, poking him in the side.

"Good! How many minutes apart are the contractions?" he asked, clearly wanting to know if he'd be able to get any more sleep.

"Five minutes, and they've been regular for almost thirty minutes."

"Five minutes!" he shouted, jumping out of bed. "Where's your suitcase?"

"Over there." I pointed to a beige leather case sitting in the corner of the room. "The clothes are probably moldy by now!"

As we left the house, Mom reminded us to call her when we knew something. We arrived at the hospital and were told I was definitely in labor. An hour later, the prep completed, I was taken to a labor room to await the birth of my second child.

"This is really great!" I kept repeating to the nurse and Al, who had been allowed in my room. "I can't believe it's this easy! Every time the pains get unbearable, someone gives me another shot and I can relax."

"It's not like the last time, is it, honey?" Al asked, bringing his chair closer to my bed.

"No, and what I like best is that you're here with me." I squeezed his hand while the next pain seared through my body. "I believe I'm getting ready to make a liar out of myself. That was no easy pain!"

The nurse checked me and told Al that he would have to leave, because in about twenty minutes he would be a father for the second time. I was wheeled into the delivery room and prepared to watch the birth of my second child; however, the local anesthetic did not take and I was put to sleep.

When I woke up, Al was bending over my bed with a Cheshire Cat grin on his face, and I knew the baby was healthy. "How long are you going to keep me in suspense?" I asked him groggily.

"Marti, it's our second boy! A big fellow weighing almost nine pounds," he said excitedly. "We have our Ronald James!" We had decided on the name while waiting in the labor room together.

"Vince has his baby brother," I murmured. "Have you called home yet?"

"Yes, and got everyone out of bed. Just think," he continued, "I'll have so much fun with our two boys..." His voice faded into the background as I embraced sleep.

CHAPTER TWENTY-SIX

September 3, 1970

Football practice had started and Al was no longer able to spend lengthy days at home. Ronnie was just a few weeks old, but the addition to the family hadn't presented any additional work so far. One beautiful late summer day, I decided to call Phyllis Loria to see if she was in the mood for a picnic.

"Hi. What are your plans for the day?" I asked after she answered the telephone.

"Nothing, really."

"How about a picnic at the park, and then maybe a run over to watch practice for a while?" I suggested.

"Sounds good. Do you want to split the stuff to bring?"

"How about if I make the sandwiches and bring the Kool-Aid? You could bring the extras," I replied, searching my bread drawer to see if I had enough bread.

"All right. I've got the car today, so I'll pick you up in about thirty minutes."

I hung up the phone and began making preparations, thinking how nice it was to have a friend who was always ready to do something on the spur of the moment. In our short acquaintance, Phyllis and I had undertaken many such adventures.

****

I met her shortly after we had moved in. Al, who coached with Phyllis' husband, Frank, suggested that I go over to their apartment and introduce myself. It seemed that Frank hadn't been coaching for too long and Phyllis was having a somewhat difficult time adjusting to his many absences. Being an early riser, I dressed Vince and myself and drove the short mile to her place about nine the next morning.

As I pulled the car into the driveway, I saw that Phyllis and Frank lived in a two-story brick apartment with a similar one adjoining it. I parked the car and went to the back entrance.

After I knocked for several minutes, a young girl with long dark hair came to the door. She was wearing her bathrobe, and I felt bad that I hadn't called her before coming over. However, she invited us in, not seeming to mind the unexpected visit.

It didn't take long before we were very much at ease with one another—partially because we had so much in common, what with our husbands being absent at the same times and our oldest children being the same age. Phyllis had two girls: Vicky, who like Vince was almost three, and anothe reighteen months younger. Vicky and Vince had quickly adjusted to each other and were busily playing in the back bedroom.

"How do you do it?" she asked, placing a coffee cup in front of me.

"Do what?"

"How do you adjust to not having Al around during sixty percent of the year? Frank is gone so much that by the time we do get to sit down together for a few minutes, I've forgotten whatever it was that I wanted to tell him."

"It's not so bad after you get used to it," I replied.

"I hope so. The days get to be so long because there's no husband coming home in the evening and nothing to look forward to." She was clearly frustrated.

"The secret is to keep busy during the daytime, so that when the evening arrives, it's pleasant to sit down and read, write or watch television."

"It only takes so much time to clean the house and do the chores," she answered.

"True! That's when you begin using your imagination by inventing various things to do. You know it can be a lot of fun."

So it was that, together, we planned our days so that the time would pass in a little more pleasant fashion.

As Frank and Al's friendship grew, so did Phyllis' and mine. When Ronnie was christened, we asked them to stand in as godparents. Heading out of the church, Al commented, "This little fellow will have a lot to live up to. Just imagine what it will be like for him to have a father who's a football coach and a godfather who not only is a football coach but also a two-time All-American football player!"

"I only hope he won't feel pressured into living up to both of you," I replied.

"Marti, I hope you'll be the first one to stop me, if ever I should push my children into athletics. Of course, I would be proud to watch them become athletes, but I'd be just as proud to see them become good at anything that might interest them," he said seriously as we approached the Lorias. "I don't even think I'd be able to coach my own children. I'd probably be too hard on them." He put Ronnie in Frank's arms.

****

Bringing my wandering mind back to the task at hand, I hurriedly packed the lunch into a Tupperware container, one I had earned by giving Tupperware parties since arriving in West Virginia. Then I gathered the children together and went out to the front porch to await Phyllis' arrival.

It had been nice of the fellows to arrange it so that one of us always had access to a car. Several of the coaches lived in the area and had formed a car pool. It was rather comical watching four large men climb into our small Volkswagon, but they never complained.

As Phyllis' yellow Ford came into view, I noticed the crumpled fender was still not repaired. A week ago I had asked her to drive me to Dunbar to pick up some Tupperware from the warehouse. On the way, we had skidded on the rain-slick interstate and had hit a wall of dirt broadside. All four of the children had been in the car, and we felt very lucky that the accident hadn't been any worse.

We had been frightened, however, and had called Frank and Al to come get us. They had climbed out of their car looking very handsome, dressed in gray shorts and green shirts, both sporting dark scowls on their faces. We had been reprimanded rather sternly, then driven home.

"We're ready!" I shouted as Phyllis opened the car door for Vince.

"I'm about to go crazy with these kids!" she answered tiredly.

"Once they get to the park, they can run off all their excess energy." I settled myself and closed the car door. "You don't look so good," I added.

"It's this lousy morning sickness," she said as we headed down Route 60.

"That'll pass. Look on the bright side—this might be the boy you've been waiting for." Like Al, Frank had been the last male bearing his family name, and both he and Phyllis were hoping for a boy this time around.

"I wouldn't mind waiting a few more years for that boy. I have a hard enough time with the two girls! Now I'm going to have another one, and all of them so close in age!"

I tried to distract her. "Remember when we all went to Frank's cabin in the spring?"

"How could I forget? We were planning on spending a few days of peace and quiet while the fellows did some of their recruiting, but when we arrived, there was no running water available!"

"And we had to lug water in buckets from the creek to the house!" I laughed.

"What do you mean, 'we'? I did the lugging—or have you forgotten that you were so pregnant you could hardly bend over to pick anything up?" she reminded me.

"Who would have guessed that you were also in your early pregnancy? All that time we were worried about keeping me from going into labor too soon, when you could easily have miscarried doing all that heavy lifting!" I paused, then grinned at another memory of the trip. "Even though the fellows weren't there very often, I did enjoy it. I still can't believe I actually had enough guts to bathe in that freezing cold water!"

"We're here," she said, parking the car with an answering smile. We busied ourselves preparing the table and setting out strict guidelines for the children to follow.

Later, after an enjoyable picnic, we all headed for the practice field to see the coaches and players in action. Everyone had high hopes for the team this year. Marshall's past record wasn't too impressive, and Rick Tolley was just beginning to get the boys into the shape he wanted them. As we pulled up to the fenced-in practice field, we saw that the boys were in the middle of drills. I searched the field in an attempt to locate Al among the flying footballs and flailing arms of players and coaches.

"I see Frank," Phyllis announced, gathering her girls together and heading in his direction.

"If I'm not ready to leave when you are, just beep the horn and we'll come back," I called to her. Carrying Ron in my arms, I began walking around the outside of the wire fence. Vince had wandered some distance ahead of me by the time I spotted Al at the opposite end of the field. He was putting his boys through some type of drill and I could hear the echo of his commanding voice.

"Vince, wait for us. I've found Daddy. Look!" And I pointed my finger in his direction.

"Can we go over there?" he asked.

"All right, but stay close to us. I wouldn't want you getting in anyone's way." By the time we reached the area, my arm was aching from holding Ronnie, so I spread out his blanket and sat down with him on the ground. Shortly, Al moved his boys to our corner of the field and had them working on some type of blocking machine.

Soon Vince noticed him and shouted, "That's my Daddy! Hi, Daddy!" Al, within earshot, did not look up to acknowledge him, but kept on shouting to his players to 'hurry up' or 'hit 'em harder!'

"Vince," I called. "Come here, honey. Daddy's working and can't be disturbed." He slowly walked back toward me with a hurt look on his face. Just as he sat down beside me, the drill broke up and Al came running over to the fence.

"Hi, Vince," he called as Vince jumped to his feet and ran to the fence. Lifting him up over it, Al tossed and tumbled with him on the ground for a minute or so. "Go back to Mommy now. Daddy has to work," he said, placing his son safely on the ground on my side of the fence. Waving to me, he ran back to his players and began another drill.

"Mommy! Daddy saw me!" Vince said happily.

It was time to leave. On our way home we passed the stadium. Although the bleachers weren't complete, the field was more or less ready for the coming season. Our first game was scheduled in two weeks, and my thoughts returned briefly to the day Al had brought me here to see it all for the first time. I was anxious for the team to do well. Phyllis and I agreed—this year we just had to have a winning season!

PART THREE

CHAPTER TWENTY-SEVEN

September 19, 1970

"Dawn, I don't want you to be concerned. It'll be a lot easier once I leave you and you're here by yourself," I said, trying to give my new babysitter more confidence. "If you should need help of any kind, one of the neighbors will be on hand. Here are their numbers." I handed her the list.

"I don't know, Marti. I feel so darn nervous," she stated as she peered down at Ronnie, barely a month old.

"You'll do just fine! After today, you'll wonder why you were ever nervous to begin with." Several weeks ago, I had engaged Dawn, a slight girl of twenty with long flowing dark hair, as my "football" babysitter. She had been given a complete list of days, nights and weekends that she would be needed during the football season. That way, there would be no last-minute hassles over finding a suitable babysitter.

When I interviewed Dawn, she had been hesitant about taking care of an infant as small as Ronnie. By talking with her, however, I could tell she'd be very good once she was on her own—but now I was beginning to think that if I didn't get out of the house soon, I would be without a sitter!

"Bye. Call me at the Tolleys' after the game if you run into any snags," I shouted, quickly climbing into my car before she could answer.

Once on the way to the stadium, I could begin to relax about the babysitting situation and worry about the other matter at hand—the game. I was never able to eat on game day until I arrived at the field, so I always left the house well before game time. Today, I was as nervous as a cat and regretted having given up cigarettes the Christmas before. "This will be a real test of strength," I thought to myself, since it would be my first football season without them.

I turned the radio on for the pre-game talk session with the coaches. Sometime soon it would be Al's turn to be interviewed, but not today. The coaches talked in circles, never committing themselves as to whether or not they expected a win.

"Of course they expect to win, you idiots!" I shouted irately at the invisible announcer. "You always expect to win! That's what it's all about!" Turning to another station, I listened to one of Al's favorite songs by the Fifth Dimension, *One Less Bell to Answer*. Shortly after it ended, I pulled into the parking lot that was set aside for the coaches and special guests.

"May I see your pass, please?" asked the tall, lanky man at the gate.

Not understanding, I asked, "What pass?"

"Ma'am, in order to park in here, you must show me a special pass," he explained patiently.

"Look, I don't know anything about a pass. All I know is that my husband coaches here and he told me this was where I was supposed to park!" I was getting more annoyed by the minute.

"I'm sorry, but..."

"Hey, Deke!" I shouted to one of the coaches passing by. He trotted over to the car. "Boy, am I glad to see you. Would you please tell this man that I'm allowed to park here? It seems Al failed to give me some kind of pass."

"It's okay. This woman is really big-league," Deke said to the attendant, using one of his favorite expressions. Deke was the oldest coach on the staff, and according to Al, knew "a helluva lot of football."

"Thanks." I pulled the VW into one of the choicest parking spaces. Several minutes later, I had my hot dog, popcorn, Coke and candy. Finding my seat, I sat down and began eating in peace, since none of the other coaches' wives had appeared yet.

Presently, Mary Jane and Cokie arrived. Mary Jane Tolley, the head coach's wife, was a tall, attractive brunette who taught high school English. Cokie was married to Shorty Moss, the offensive coordinator and the man Al worked under. Everyone who looked at Cokie was instantly attracted by her almost-black hair and deep brown eyes. Her daughter, Aundrea, was six months younger than Vince.

"Hi," they greeted me in unison.

"Have a seat. It looks like we're going to have a good turnout for our first game." I beckoned for them to sit down.

"I guess so. I wonder how hard it will be to get out afterwards." Mary Jane stressed the word "out" with a very Virginia accent.

"Are you going to Mary Jane's after the game?" asked Cokie, settling herself properly on the bleacher.

"Sure. Isn't everyone?" I asked Mary Jane.

"Only those people who hear about it. We didn't send out invitations, because we wanted only friends and supporters to show up," she answered. "If there's anyone you want to bring, you'll have to tell them about it."

"There's nobody," I said, turning my attention to the players doing their pre-game exercises. Shortly, Phyllis Loria arrived and I moved my coat to let her sit in the seat I had saved for her.

"Late again! The babysitter didn't arrive on time and I had to park several blocks away," she said disgustedly.

"Why didn't you tell me you needed a ride? I would have been happy to pick you up." I shielded my eyes against the bright sunlight. "You'd think the home side wouldn't be facing the blasted sun!"

"I'd never get organized fast enough to leave when you do," she answered. "Guess Frank will be up in the box today."

"Looks like they're about ready. The band is forming on the sidelines." I noticed Al down by the team's bench, earphones wrapped over his ears.

"Yeah!" shouted Mary Jane and Cokie as the team came running onto the field. Following suit, Phyllis and I cheered loudly. At halftime, the score was close, but Marshall was ahead and remained so throughout the entire game—our first victory.

"I'm so happy we won!" I stood up to stretch the kinks out of my body. "Anyone going down to the field house to see the fellows?"

"I've got to get home and do a little organizing before everyone arrives," said Mary Jane, retrieving her purse from beneath her seat. Cokie and Phyllis had other places to go, too, so I was left alone. I thought it strange that they didn't want to greet their husbands after the game. Walking toward the field house, I paused, wondering if I should go on alone. Never had I asked Al how he felt about me showing up there after a game, win or lose.

In the end, I decided to do as the other wives did, and headed on up to Mary Jane's. Until then, I hadn't realized how much seeing Al after the games meant to me. As I traveled up the winding mountain road to the Tolleys' house, I made a mental note to ask him about it.

I was one of the first to arrive, which gave me a few minutes to myself. I called Dawn to make sure she was getting along all right, and found that she was enjoying herself with the boys. After Mary Jane gave me a tour of the house, I settled down in the bar area with a post-game drink. When the men arrived in force, laughing and excited, I approached Al.

"Congratulations!" I said and gave him a hug.

"I looked for you after the game. Where were you?" he asked. I knew then that he enjoyed our few quiet moments together after a game as much as I did. I was disappointed that I hadn't followed my intuition and gone down to the field house.

"I wasn't sure if you wanted me to be the only wife down there, so I stayed away. I really wanted to come, but thought I should ask you about it first."

"Honey, I always want you to be there—win or lose," he said, giving my chin a gentle shove.

The remainder of the evening was spent discussing glorious plans for future wins. Everyone was delighted that the season's opener had put our record at 1-0.

CHAPTER TWENTY-EIGHT

October 3, 1970

"You have all the directions: what to feed the children, where we're going to be, and when we'll be returning," I reminded Dawn as I excitedly gathered together my clothes and suitcase and hurried out the back door.

"Have a good time, Marti, and don't worry about a thing," she reassured me.

"There was a time when I might have worried myself sick over leaving the children behind, but not anymore!" I replied, getting into the car and starting the motor. "See you when I get back."

I could hardly believe it! For the first time in our married life, Al and I were going to be together for a whole night and two days without the children, provided Al would be allowed to stay over with me after the game rather than returning with the team on the bus. It was such a beautiful day that I refused to think it might not all work out the way I hoped.

We were playing Xavier College that evening and the stadium was located in the Cincinnati area. I had recently learned that one of my favorite sorority sisters was living there with her husband, also a graduate of Lenoir Rhyne. Al and I had known both of them, but hadn't seen either one since we were in college. I had to laugh when I remembered how I had called Sandra as soon as I found out we were playing there.

****

It was late one evening when I impulsively picked up the telephone and dialed her number.

"Hello," came Sandra's musical voice from the other end of the line.

"Hello, Mrs. Eades. This is Mrs. Smith of Brown's Paving Contractors, and I am calling to confirm the delivery of one thousand pounds of cement to 6501 Brackenridge tomorrow morning at seven a.m. sharp," I said, trying to disguise my voice.

"Cement! I don't know anything about cement! Steveeeeee!" she began shouting hysterically for her husband.

"Sandra! Sandra!" I switched back to my normal husky voice. "It's just a joke," I laughed. "This is Marti Bergstresser Carelli."

"Marti! You rat! Where in the world are you?" she asked, at the same time trying to explain to Steve what was happening.

"I'm in Huntington, West Virginia. Al is the line coach at Marshall University."

"Hey, that's great! We'll have to get together sometime. We haven't seen any Lenoir Rhyne people in years!" she exclaimed.

"Well, that's sort of why I'm calling. In several weeks we're playing Xavier, and I thought maybe I could leave early in the morning and get there in plenty of time to visit. I'll get some tickets for the two of you and then you could escort me to the game. If we're lucky, Al might be persuaded to spend the night there and leave early the next morning," I proposed, inviting myself as usual.

"Marti, that sounds great! We'll definitely plan on it!"

"I'll plan on coming, then, and if you don't hear from me again, I'll be there." After we exchanged telephone numbers and addresses, I said, "I'll save all our talking for when I arrive. Take care and I'll see you soon."

****

"Yipes!" I shouted as my car headed toward a tree, forcing my mind back to the present. It was getting near lunchtime so I pulled into a nearby restaurant. As I walked in, I noticed people staring at me, and wondered if it was really so unusual for someone to be wearing a fringed suede ensemble. In Chapel Hill it would have gone unnoticed, but in Kentucky or West Virginia I supposed it was an oddity.

After eating, I had only a short distance to go and arrived on schedule. I stopped at the gas station Sandra had indicated and called her number so she could meet me and lead me to her house. Fifteen minutes later, she pulled up in a dark Cadillac, and I thought as I saw her that she had not changed a lick in five years.

We spent the afternoon in constant chatter, trying to catch up on all that had happened since the "good old days." It was soon time to leave for the game, and Steve escorted us to the car.

We arrived before the kickoff. As we took our seats, I greeted several loyal Marshall fans who had come to watch the game.

"I'm so nervous!" I exclaimed, sitting down with my Scotch plaid cape wrapped around my shoulders.

"No sweat," said Steve. "You'll win tonight. I can feel it."

"Don't tell me you're psychic!" I said teasingly.

"Sure. I'll tell you when we'll have a touchdown, a fumble, or whatever you desire to know," he replied seriously. I was so gullible that I didn't know whether to believe him or not, but finally decided against it.

"Not to change the subject, but Al did look terrific last night, and the other coach he was with, Frank Loria, was beautiful." Sandra's wide smile revealed her dimples and Hollywood teeth.

"That was a nice visit we had with them at the house last evening," put in Steve. He had told me earlier that I was some lucky woman to have found Al.

At that time, the team came onto the field and we turned our attention to the game that followed. Steve had been right in his "feeling," for we did come away the winners.

We climbed down from the bleachers to wait for Al to come out of the dressing rooms. The wait wasn't as long as usual, and my weekend dreams came true when he told me we could stay until the next morning. Together we returned to the house, where Sandra fixed a midnight dinner. Pleasantly exhausted, Al and I retired for the evening, packing before we went to sleep.

Early the next morning we left Sandra and Steve's house. As we waved goodbye to their two small boys, replicas of our own, I wondered if our next meeting would take place before another five years had passed.

Although it wasn't as sunny as the day before, it seemed bright to us as we traveled the miles toward home. Even knowing that we were on a tight schedule—Al had to be at a meeting in the early afternoon—didn't make us feel pressured; we passed the morning talking of whatever popped into our heads. When I asked Al the question, it startled even me.

"What would you do if I should die?" I snuggled as close to him as the gear shift allowed.

"I guess I've never thought about it," he answered as his face furrowed into a frown. "Why?"

"I don't know. It's just that we should probably talk about it." I couldn't believe what I was saying, because I had always hated discussing death, especially around men who were selling insurance policies. "What would you do about the children?"

"I guess I'd ask my mother to come stay with them until I could hire a permanent housekeeper or something."

"You wouldn't ever send them away to stay with your mom, would you?" I asked, turning to look at him. "If I should die, then they would need their father more than ever."

"No, honey, I wouldn't send them away," he laughed and tickled my knee.

"Where would you bury me?" I asked, not amused.

"You're really persistent, aren't you?" He began to settle down and take our conversation more seriously. "I don't know. Where would you like to be buried?"

"Actually, I'd rather be cremated, but now that I'm Catholic, I guess that's out of the question," I said, briefly remembering my confirmation into the church on our third wedding anniversary, a year and a half ago. The decision had been entirely mine and Al had been completely surprised. "I don't care where I'm buried, really. I'll leave that up to you."

"In that case, I'd probably bury you in New Jersey," he said as if a difficult decision had been made.

"This may sound ridiculous and contradictory, but would you promise me one thing?"

"I can't promise anything until I know what it is."

"I'm serious, so I don't want you laughing at me when I tell you," I pleaded.

"All right. All right. I won't laugh." He pressed his lips tightly together, determined to hold in any laughter.

"If I should die, no matter how many other wives you have, I want to be the one who's buried beside you," I said, stumbling over the words in an attempt to get them out quickly.

"That should be easy enough," he said. I was relieved that he hadn't laughed.

"With my insurance money, you ought to be able to bury me and hire a housekeeper for about a year. How long do you think it would take you to get married again? Even though I don't like to think about it now, I do want Vince and Ron to have a mother to take care of them." I continued, now on a tangent, "You'll have to be sure she really loves them!" I had a feeling that, with me out of the picture, women would come flocking to his door.

"What about you?" Al said, turning the topic of discussion in my direction.

"What do you mean, 'what about you?'" I asked, stretching my feet out and placing my head on his right shoulder.

"What would you do if I were the one to die?"

"I don't know...be completely lost," I said.

"You're much too independent to be completely lost," he said firmly. "Really, what would you do?"

"The first thing I'd do is leave Huntington."

"Why?" he asked as he slowed the car for a new speed zone.

"Why in the world would I stay here? Both our families are miles and miles away, and I haven't lived here long enough to feel that this is anything but a temporary home," I answered heatedly, the subject beginning to get on my nerves.

"Where would you go?"

"I suppose I'd just travel around until I found a little town that I liked, move in, get a job and attempt to start living again."

"Wait a minute! Since we're spelling out stipulations, I have one for you," Al said and looked at me sideways. "I wouldn't want you to work again until the boys were in school. You've already been away from Vince more than I've been happy about."

"All right. Any others?" I asked. "Where would you like to be buried?"

"I suppose New Jersey, since that's where I'm burying you." He avoided any further comments on the subject of my being buried beside him. "You'd have an adequate insurance policy to keep you going for a while."

"I doubt that I'd get married again for a long time."

"I'm not worried about you. Some nice guy would come along and rescue you," he teased.

"I'm not about to go around hanging out in those bars you're always talking about, so I don't see how any nice fellow would ever be able to find me among the diapers and dirty wash," I said with a quiver in my voice. The once-interesting subject had become terribly depressing and I just wanted to forget the whole thing.

"Honey, are you crying?" Al turned my face toward his and saw the tears streaming down my cheeks.

"It's just that I don't want to talk about this anymore," I sniffed.

"Sad movies, sad songs, sad stories—they all make you cry. You're so sentimental, baby, but I wouldn't have you any other way." He squeezed my shoulder in an effort to comfort me.

We drove in peace for the remainder of the journey and arrived at the gymnasium right on schedule. After letting Al out to join Shorty, who was approaching the entrance, I turned the car toward home. I had missed the children and could hardly wait to see them. As I pulled into the gravel driveway, I saw Vince playing in the yard.

"Hi!" I greeted him, handing him a small bag to carry into the house.

"Did you enjoy yourself?" asked Dawn as she took my cape and skirt from my arms.

"It was lovely, just lovely!" I answered, the excitement bubbling within me. "It was just one beautiful weekend!" I repeated and felt peace surrounding me.

CHAPTER TWENTY-NINE

October 24, 1970

"Yeah!" The crowds cheered as the players' parents stepped out onto the field to welcome them. It was Homecoming and the game had been nip-and-tuck from the beginning. As the halftime show ended, I called to one of the other coaches' daughters.

"Here's the camera. What I want you to do is to go down near the wall and snap as many pictures as you can. Try to catch Al when he's off-guard," I instructed, handing over the instamatic camera.

I had been wanting to get a few candid shots of Al during a game, but knew that it would embarrass him if he ever saw me doing it, so I employed Coach Koker's oldest daughter instead. As the game progressed, I kept my eye on her to see that she was following my directions. From what I saw, it appeared that I would be getting some very successful slides.

The whole day had been gorgeous, with the sun at full strength and the temperature mild. I felt attractive in my new homemade red dress, black high-top vinyl boots, and french curl hairdo. For this game, I had splurged and gone to the hairdresser, something I did only once or twice a year. At Al's request, I had begun sewing again, and had made an entire wardrobe for football season. The dress I was wearing was his favorite, mainly because it was short and red. It pleased him to see me in that color with a lot of my extra-long legs showing.

As the game continued, it became evident that we would lose. So far, our season hadn't been too bad, but it could have been great since the games we lost were close until the finish. But "could-have-beens" never counted, as Al always reminded me. It was no use rehashing something that was in the past.

Keeping this in mind, I approached the field house after the game. I was still the only wife who went there, but I never minded, knowing that Al approved. It was still very muddy because of the construction in that area, so I paused to wait on a board that had been placed across an extremely large puddle.

"Hi, Marti. How's that new baby of yours?" I turned to greet Jim Gilbert, who I had met shortly after our move to Huntington. At that time, he was working with the football team in order to earn enough money to finish college. He had once played football for Marshall, but had taken some time off to join the Army Reserves before finishing college. Al had brought him to the house several times for dinner, and he always seemed the typical extroverted football player, sporting the physique of a back rather than a lineman.

"Oh, he's growing like a weed," I answered, and in order to keep the conversation from dragging, continued, "I've seen you at just about every game. What do you do, drive over here from Columbus every weekend?"

"I never miss a game, if I can help it."

"Do you miss coaching, or has the business world gotten its hold on you?" I asked him as the boys began silently piling out of the field house on their way to the bus.

"Sure, I miss it, but I need to give that business world you speak of a little more time before I'll know if it's for me." I could see Al at the doorway, but he was talking with some of the men, so I remained where I was.

"Are you coming up to Coach Tolley's after the game?" I asked Jim.

"I haven't been invited."

"No one is ever invited. You just show up if you feel like it."

"I'd feel more comfortable if Rick had told me about it," he answered, trying to brush his windblown brown hair into place with his right hand.

"Well, if you need an invitation, then I'm giving you one. You're welcome to come if you feel like it." I hurried to meet Al, who had broken away from the group.

"How long do you think you'll be?" I asked Al as he walked me to the car a few minutes later.

"At least an hour or so," he responded, closing the door for me.

"I'm going back to the house for a minute before I pick up Phyllis, so we should both be arriving at about the same time. Bye, hon. I'm sorry about the game," I said and backed out of the parking lot.

Al had really been down after this game—it had been a hard one to lose. There were only three games left in the season, and Marshall had to win them all to come out ahead. The following week was our last home game, with the other two being played out of state. The coaches had been pleased that they had been able to afford the charter of a Southern Airways Jetliner to transport the boys to the East Carolina game. In past years, they had to suffer through hours of bus riding before reaching their destination.

Pushing all thoughts of future games from my mind, I made my necessary stops and headed toward Mary Jane's house, prepared for a dull evening dampened by our loss.

When Phyllis and I arrived, we were amazed at all the people present.

Usually, after a losing game, people went elsewhere to party. "We might as well make the best of it," I commented to Phyllis as I headed for the coat closet.

Phyllis scanned the room. "The coaches aren't here yet."

"No, and I doubt if they're in any hurry to arrive, either." Doing our best, we began to mingle. Half an hour later I was relieved to see Rick come through the front door, followed by Al, Red, Deke, Karl, Frank, and Shorty.

"Don't look so depressed," I said to Al as I punched him playfully in the stomach. "These are your friends."

"That's what you think! These friends are the ones who will be the first to suggest firing you if you begin losing," he said under his breath. I took another look to see onetime friends turned enemies.

"No wonder so many coaches have ulcers and heart problems."

"I suppose I'd better give the other guys a break and take my turn at hearing the criticism," he said, walking toward the crowd. I knew how much he would rather be at home, shut away in some room, and felt sorry that what he loved doing the most in the whole world was full of so many pressures.

Since I wasn't the most diplomatic person around, I knew that Al wouldn't leave me alone for long. Several minutes later, I saw him steering Jim Gilbert in my direction.

"If you don't mind, would you please stand here with my wife and keep her company until I can get back to her?" he asked, and turned to me. "I've been telling Jim he's been dating the wrong broad, but he claims he struck out with the one I recommended!" Al teased and I was grateful to see that the worst of his mood was over.

"I hope you don't mind being my chaperone, but Al knows I can't abide this mingling business, and I suppose he doesn't trust what I'll say if someone should come right out with a direct criticism of the coaches. I've been known to 'bop' a few spectators," I rambled. Jim only smiled at my comment. Whether the poor guy liked it or not, he was stuck with me for a while.

"Hi, baby, you look mighty nice tonight," crooned one of the other female guests a bit tipsily. "Are you old enough for me?"

"How old is old enough?" Jim asked, coolly playing her little game. I had to laugh to myself as I remembered Al telling Shorty once that he never had to figure out whether another woman was flirting with him or not, because if I thought she was, I would be at his side in a minute, and that would be his clue to withdraw gracefully.

While my mind wandered, I must have missed something, because when I looked back at Jim, the woman was gone.

"What happened?" I asked curiously.

"I was too young for her," he laughed.

"How old are you?" I thought Al had told me he was somewhere in the neighborhood of twenty-eight.

"I'll be twenty-four in February. Would you like me to fix you another drink?" he asked politely.

"All right," I said. I had only been drinking ginger ale, a trick I used quite often since alcohol was not my pleasure. "Why hasn't some woman grabbed you before now?" I was always interested in how eligible bachelors could ward off complete entanglement.

"I just haven't been as fortunate as Al, Shorty or the rest of the coaches in finding someone who would understand my involvement in athletics as much as you women do," he replied quite seriously. His comment impressed me, probably because it reflected favorably on me.

"Are you ready?" asked Al, coming up behind us. He and I collected our coats and headed for the car.

"Have I told you how sexy you look?" he asked, pretending to attack me as we got into the VW.

"Only once," I said, hinting for another compliment.

"You should wear your hair that way more often. It's very becoming."

"Thank you. I like it too, but to get it this way, I had to sit in the beauty parlor for four hours to the tune of twelve dollars!"

"Wow! I guess I'll like it just as well hanging all over your shoulders."

"Do we have time to stop at the Makiki for a drink?"

"Don't you just want to go home?" he asked, sounding tired.

"No! I would like to be with you alone, surrounded by candlelight," I answered, beginning to pout for fear that he would say no.

"All right, just for half an hour," he relented. "I guess it's natural to want to be seen when you've gone to so much trouble to look nice." And I felt silly that he had seen right through some of my own feelings.

As it turned out, the minute we entered the club and were shown to our table for two, people began swarming around to comment on various aspects of the afternoon's game. It took us more than an hour to slip away from them, but I enjoyed watching the smooth manner in which Al handled himself. The hour hadn't been a total waste, for even though people had been around us, we held hands underneath the table, and with our eyes sent messages that we both understood. It was good to reach the privacy of our home.

CHAPTER THIRTY

November 5, 1970

"About what time will you be home?" I asked Al as he closed his briefcase.

"The school isn't too far away. I suppose Frank and I will get back to Huntington around 11:30 this evening. We may even leave by halftime; it'll all depend on how impressed we are with the boys we'll be scouting," he answered and took his overcoat from the overcrowded closet.

"I doubt that I'll wait up, then. I'm really sleepy enough to go to bed now." I kissed him goodbye and turned my attention to Vince, who had just darted into the bathroom with something bulging from beneath his shirt.

"What are you playing with, Vince?" I went into the bathroom and confronted him. "Well, what is it?"

"It's just what Daddy and that man gave me," he said, pulling an empty film reel out from beneath his undershirt. Last Sunday, Al had taken Vince with him to pick up the films from the previous game. They had so few times together that I was delighted to see the two of them drive off.

"Honey, you're allowed to play with that. The man gave it to you, so don't act so guilty about it," I told him and began undressing him for an early bath.

By seven-thirty, both children were in bed and an empty evening lay ahead. I was not in the mood to do any more sewing or letter writing, so about the only recourse left was to begin another book. Last night, Al had come home to find me in tears, with *Love Story* open on my lap. He had made me sit down beside him and tell him the whole sad story, after which he had comforted me and put me to bed. Now, I replaced it in the bookcase and withdrew a volume that was certain to contain a light, happy tale. I curled up in bed, pillows piled high behind me, and began reading. By ten-thirty I had turned out the lights and gone off to sleep.

The shrill sound of the telephone beside my bed jarred me from a pleasant dream back to reality. I looked over at the illuminated face of the clock radio and noticed it was one-thirty in the morning. Upon awakening, I had realized that Al wasn't home yet. On the fifth or sixth ring, I picked up the pale blue receiver and said, "Hello."

"Marti, is Al home yet?" asked Phyllis, sounding rather upset.

"No, he isn't," I answered.

"Where could they be? This is really making me angry; I thought they were going to be home by midnight."

"Al mentioned a similar time, but don't get all uptight about it. They probably stopped somewhere for a drink or a bite to eat and the time just slipped away. You know how they are—time means nothing when they're having fun!" I tried to reassure her. "Doesn't some relative of yours own a bar in Charleston?"

Her voice rising, she said, "Yes, and if Frank's there he'll be locked out of this house, that's for sure!"

"I wouldn't worry about it. They probably did stop there," I said, telling her I'd call if I heard anything and that she should do the same.

After hanging up the telephone, I went into the kitchen and made some coffee. I was in no mood to sleep. The more I thought about the lateness of the hour, the more worried I became.

"Damn it! If you knew you were going to be late, why didn't you at least call me?" I muttered aloud to myself. I tried to push more frightening thoughts from my mind by concentrating on the hell I'd give Al for being so inconsiderate, but it was no use. I began to worry seriously about him being involved in a car accident.

I had never expressed my deep concern for him whenever he was on the road traveling, because traveling was part of his job and I didn't want to add any additional burdens. I was always relieved whenever he was able to fly instead of drive, because then I never worried about his safety.

Taking my coffee into the living room, I turned out the lights, sat on the sofa and waited. It was inevitable that my imagination would eventually run wild, and I became convinced that Al had been in a car wreck and was either dead or in critical condition. Numbly, I waited for the ring of the telephone to confirm my thoughts.

By three o'clock, the waiting had become unbearable and I was practically in hysterics. I paced the floor, wringing my hands and crying, all the while pretending that he would come walking through the door, and all the sickening feelings that had caught in my stomach would disappear in a rush of relief.

Taking hold of myself, I sat down on the hassock in front of the picture window, looking out into the dimly-lit street. The sensation of my stomach turning over at the sight of every approaching car was more comforting than the darkness of the shadowy living room. Then it happened—the squatty VW pulled slowly into the driveway, and Al came walking swiftly to the door. He was startled to see me as he opened it.

"Where have you been?" I asked in a calm voice that disguised the anger I felt welling up inside me.

"I'm sorry I'm late, but Frank and I stopped in Charleston on our way home and the time just slipped by," he explained, dumping his coat and briefcase into the nearest chair. "I'm tired. Let's get to bed."

"You're tired!" I screamed at him, the anger emerging full force. "The next time you tell me you're going to be home by eleven-thirty but don't show up until three-thirty, you'd better have the damn decency to call me! I've been sitting here for hours worrying myself sick, thinking you'd been killed in some damn car wreck!" I ran into the bedroom, slamming the door.

"Marti, don't be so loud. You'll wake the children," he cautioned, coming into the bedroom as I got under the covers. "Look, I'm sorry you were worried, but you should know that you'd be the first to be informed if something happened to me."

"How can you say that for certain? You probably don't even have our home phone number on you!" I retaliated. Turning over, I fell asleep before he was in bed. It was the first time that we hadn't discussed a disagreement or misunderstanding immediately after it happened, but sleep came easily because I was so relieved that he was safely home.

CHAPTER THIRTY-ONE

November 7, 1970

Everyone screamed for joy as the buzzer went off, signifying the end of the game.

"Thank God for that one!" exclaimed Mary Jane as she smiled brightly and clasped her hands together. "Now I've got to get busy." Energetically, she departed for home and her party preparations.

"Do you mind meeting me at the car? I want to see Al," I said to Phyllis.

"That's fine. We probably won't be staying long this evening, because Frank has promised to take me out to dinner!" she replied cheerfully. "I'm still angry with him over the other night, and this is his way of apologizing."

"I won't be too long," I promised. When I reached the field house, the coaches were still milling around outside excitedly talking to some fans.

"We did it!" Al shouted, giving me a crushing squeeze. "At halftime I wasn't so sure what the outcome was going to be."

"I never give up hope, but you were playing a rather lousy game the first half." I stopped with that little bit of observation, having learned a long time before that it wasn't wise to criticize the decisions the coaches made during the crucial moments of a game.

"I was really touched by our men at halftime," he said. "We'd been so disgusted with their playing that all we did was break up into our little groups and let them sit alone in silence. Then one of the men got up under his own steam and gave a pep talk, ending with, 'This time we're gonna go out there and win for the coaches!' and they did!"

"They certainly seemed psyched up when they came onto the field," I remarked.1

"We'll be up to the party soon, but first we have to meet with some newspapermen. It sure is gratifying to win our last home game!" Al said, motioning to a fellow coach that he would be along in a minute.

"I've got to go too, so I'll see you in a little while."

"Okay." He left me and approached the men, shaking each one's hand vigorously. I was happy to see him in such high spirits.

When I finally arrived at the Tolleys' home, the party was in full swing. Someone had brought along a recording of the university's fight song, and they were preparing to play it when the coaches came in. I found my way over to a table heaped with delicious dips, meats and sweets.

"Hi, Cokie," I greeted Shorty's wife.

"Are you planning to go to the East Carolina game?" she asked me.

"I don't know. Al said a decision hasn't been made on whether to take all the wives."

"Shorty wants me to go, but I haven't decided if I want to spend all that money for a one-night trip. Besides, our bowling team is entered in a tournament this Saturday, and Elaine, our captain, is flying to the game. I don't think it's wise for two of us to be absent from the team."

"I didn't know the wives had to pay," I commented.

"As far as I know, we do."

"I'll have to remember to ask Al about it. I love to fly."

"What are you up to?" asked Phyllis as she tried to squeeze her heavily-pregnant body around the end of the table where the bread was located.

"Are you planning to fly to the game next weekend?" I knifed a piece of dried beef.

"I really doubt it. I haven't felt too well through this entire pregnancy, and I'd most likely be tired out before we got started."

"You'd better not fill yourself up, nibbling like that!" I teased her. "If you really want to make Frank pay for being late the other night, you'll have to be able to eat the best filet mignon on the menu!"

"Don't worry! I most certainly will!" she laughed.

"Here they come," shouted one of the guests from across the room.

"I'd better go see about that record," said Cokie, heading for the stereo.

The moment the coaches came through the door, *We Are the Sons of Marshall* blared through the speakers. Everyone joined the men as they began clapping and forming a circle. Our voices blended with those on the record, and a loud roar went up as the song came to an end. It would most definitely be a lively night!

At about ten o'clock Al told me he had a surprise planned and I should be ready to leave in half an hour. When the time came, he confided that he had made reservations at the Makiki for a late dinner for two. Needless to say, I was delighted.

Once we arrived, we were promptly escorted to a table right in the center of the room near the band. When I saw the direction in which we were headed, I feared that the evening would be a repetition of the week before. However, I was pleasantly surprised, for even though we nodded to several neighbors and friends, not one soul interrupted our dinner or conversation.

"You know, I've always been proud to say that you are my wife," Al said softly, in trend with the things he had been saying all evening. "I've never been disappointed in you—you've never let me down." I just listened, savoring the compliments that I knew were often thought but seldom expressed.

"Honey, I've always loved you and each day that passes, it grows stronger. Sometimes I feel that if it got more powerful, I'd just burst wide open," I replied, caressing his strong hands.

For the next few hours, we reminisced about our dating days and laughed about the misunderstandings we'd had during our four and a half years of marriage. I was aware that Al regretted not calling me the other night to let me know he was going to be late, and felt that our evening's conversation had been prompted by that.

Before leaving, we danced to the songs *Sunny* and *More*, favorites from our college days. Our moods and the atmosphere had blended together into an emotional evening filled with expressions of the love that was in our hearts. It was an evening never to be forgotten.

CHAPTER THIRTY-TWO

November 13, 1970

It was cold. There was a woman standing alone. The colors were bright—red, yellow, and white, lots of white. They were turning in front of the woman. No, no they were not! They were still. They were flowers. People. They laughed. The woman seemed confused. They were crying. It was a black woman. No. It was a black coat. She was wearing a black coat, a black hat, black boots. I observed the woman. She was not crying. Her stomach hurt. It was raw, maybe. No. It felt like it was raw inside. Her sickness engulfed me—the woman was me. I was crying, but my cheeks were dry. The flowers came closer and closer. They were on top of brown mud. It was windy—dusty. The flowers blew away. It was not mud! It was a brown box on top of mud. No! No! I shook my head. I tried to run but my arms and legs stayed in place. I cried. My cheeks were wet. It was a box. It was a coffin—Al's coffin.

"Marti! Marti! Wake up!" shouted Al. I felt him shaking me.

"What's the matter?" I mumbled, trying to figure out why I was in bed and not running away.

"Honey, you were shouting 'no, no' in your sleep. I think you were even crying." I touched my face and felt the tears on my cheeks.

"It was horrible! I had a dream that I was at your funeral!"

"Marti, honey, calm down. It was only a dream. Look at me. I'm here! Come on, touch me, and believe it was nothing but a bad dream," he said as I turned into his embrace. "Come on, it's the middle of the night. Forget about it and let's go to sleep."

I did forget. It would be several weeks later, while I cradled Ronnie in the wee hours of the morning, that I would remember and know my nightmare had come true.

At the time, however, I drifted into a peaceful sleep and woke up the next morning ready to dig into my housecleaning.

"Call me today if you have any free time, but <u>do</u> <u>not</u> come home until supper time," I cautioned Al. I wanted to have the house in order for tonight's party.

"What time will that be?"

"I don't know. Whenever you get hungry. I was hoping I could get out of cooking—that maybe you'd be kind enough to bring home some hamburgers and french fries."

"What kind of party are you having this time?" he asked.

"It's a toy party, kind of like my Tupperware parties. With Christmas around the corner, it's the perfect time to have one." I put the last breakfast dish away and began assembling my cleaning aids.

"I thought you already had all our Christmas presents bought and wrapped."

"I do! Aren't you proud of me? Actually, I'm hoping this party will earn me a peg table for Vince. Oh! Have I shown you what I got for us to give him for his birthday next week?" I asked excitedly.

"No."

"Wait just a minute, and I'll go fetch it!" I hurried into our bedroom, opened the closet door and rummaged behind shoes until I found it. "Look. It's a red portable record player," I said, showing it to Al as I entered the kitchen.

"That's nice. He'll have a lot of fun with it. By the way, don't touch my suitcase. I packed it early this morning, and I'll just pick it up before leaving for the airport."

"What time are you taking off?" I asked as I gave him a hug.

"Around seven."

"I've invited all of the wives tonight, so at least we'll be busy."

"You'll stay out of trouble that way," he joked. "Gotta go. I'll call before I come home, so you'll be able to remind me about those hamburgers."

As I watched the car drive out of sight, I wished I were going to the game with Al. In the middle of the week, he had told me they'd decided that if all the wives couldn't go, none of us would. I remembered replying without thought, "I guess that's just as well. If your plane should crash like the Wichita team's did, then one of us would still be around to take care of the children."

It was a weird thing to have said, but the recent crash of the Wichita team's plane had hit home. I had found myself, day in and day out, searching the papers for details about the survivors.

"Stop daydreaming and get to work," I muttered and poured myself another cup of coffee. Even after the Wichita disaster, I felt no apprehension about this flying trip. The Southern jets were very safe and had flown Carolina's teams before.

At five o'clock, Al called and reported that he would be home shortly. I surveyed the house and was pleased. Everything was ready when he arrived bearing gifts.

"What's this for?" I asked as he handed me two small, nicely-wrapped boxes.

"It's your belated birthday present," he said, a little shyly. My birthday had been two weeks before, and had slipped his mind entirely. He remembered it while carrying out the garbage two days after the event, and I heard him mutter, "I wish I were dead!" I hadn't been upset about his forgetfulness, because after twenty-seven years of birthdays, I was beginning to wish that I could forget them myself.

"They're lovely!" I exclaimed, happily showing off my matching leather wallet and key chain. "Thank you, honey!"

"I had them picked out for some time, but just never got around to going after them," he said. "Look, I see John outside. I'd best go say goodbye before I have to leave. Vince, come on, I'll take you for a ride on my shoulders."

John and Doris Hanley had been our next-door neighbors since we had moved in, and were natives of Huntington. Having received a promotion, John was leaving in the morning for Missouri, while Doris was to remain behind for several weeks. I watched from the kitchen window as Al talked with John and played with Vince. Then I heard Frank's car horn beep and hollered out the back door to Al.

"Frank is here," I called, clearing up the baby's dish and empty bottles. Al went to get his suitcase, briefcase and coat.

"How do I look?" he asked. I held him at arm's length and looked him up and down.

"Very handsome, I must admit! You're wearing the entire outfit that you won at the golf tournament," I observed. Several months before, at a coaches' gathering, Al's name had been drawn and he'd won a gift certificate at a local men's store. With it he had gotten a suit, shirt, tie, belt and cuff links. "Brown definitely suits you."

"Vince, come give me a kiss before I go," Al said. Vince jumped up into his arms and placed his head on his father's shoulder, then scrambled down. "Where's Ronnie?"

"I'll get him from his crib. Time for bed, you know." I brought him out into the living room, and Al took him from me.

"Come on, big fellow, give your daddy a little smile," he said, gently pinching his son's soft cheeks. "You've changed so much that I hardly recognize you." Ronnie laughed. "You don't know me now, but I'll make up for it later," Al ended. Lifting him high, he brushed his lips against Ronnie's cheek.

"Bye, honey," he said and kissed me.

"Bye," I responded, thinking, "Good luck," a term I never used aloud before any game for fear of jinxing it.

After putting Ronnie back in his crib, I went to the front window, watching Al pause at the mailbox to talk briefly with a neighbor. Suddenly, I had a strong urge to hold him once more. Aware that he would think it strange for me to say goodbye again, I picked up Vince as my excuse and walked out into the front yard.

"Al, Vince wanted to give you one more kiss," I said, handing over our son and pressing my body against Al's. After embracing him, I turned to go back into the house.

"Hey, Marti!" Frank called to me from his car. "Don't you know it's bad luck to have a party on Friday the thirteenth?" he teased.

"No, that's my lucky number, but if you're superstitious, you'd best take out lots of flight insurance," I retorted.

Al, who had almost gotten into the front seat, backed out and stood up. Characteristically gesturing, he joked, "Don't worry, babe! If anything should happen to me, you'll have enough insurance money to be well taken care of!" He climbed back into the car. As they drove off, I thought about the term insurance notice lying on Al's desk. It would expire in several weeks, and I had forgotten to ask him if he wanted it renewed.

Walking back to the house, my thoughts turned to other matters. A few short moments ago, I had hugged Al—but as I put Vince to bed, I was unaware that it was the last embrace we would ever share.

CHAPTER THIRTY-THREE

November 13, 1970

"Now this toy is one of the most unique that we have." The demonstrator pulled a red race car out of a nearby box. "It doesn't run on batteries, which ought to please all of you mothers! If you pull this extended strip of plastic, the car will race off in any direction you want it to, and when it hits an object, it'll bounce off and turn in another direction."

As she proceeded to demonstrate, I politely left the room to prepare the brownies and coffee that I had made. It had been a nice gathering of about fifteen people and everyone seemed to be enjoying themselves. I peered around the corner to see what was happening, and saw that the demonstration was finished and my guests were examining the toys.

"If anyone is thirsty or hungry, there's food in the kitchen," I shouted above the noise of excited voices.

"I'm ready for some coffee," stated Jean, the graduate assistant coach's wife. "Boy, those brownies look delicious!"

"I'm glad you're going to be able to stay over tonight," I said. "I wish my children were old enough to stay for a visit with their grandparents."

"It's a nice break," Jean answered, her dimples prominent as she spoke.

"Say, are you going to be able to stay tomorrow afternoon to listen to the game with me?"

"I don't see why not. Gail won't be flying back with the team, so he won't get home until the next morning," she said, pouring a cup of coffee for one of my neighbors.

"I suppose that I'd better go into the living room to see how everyone's doing. Anyway, we'll have all night to talk." I spent the next few hours visiting with my friends, and by eleven-thirty everyone had gone home except Jean,

Dawn, and the demonstrator.

"Are you certain Billy isn't going to get cold feet?" I teased Dawn, who was engaged to a man in the service. The wedding had been planned for December, only a short time after he was to arrive home.

"I don't think he will, but I might!" she laughed. I had always enjoyed Dawn's company and welcomed her visits.

"I know one thing—I'll never be able to find a babysitter to replace you," I said, reluctantly thinking about all the trouble I'd have to go to when she did get married.

"I'm sure you'll find someone very suitable," she soothed.

For the next hour we drank coffee and ate more brownies. Finally, at about twelve-thirty, Jean and I were left alone.

"Are you about ready for bed?" I asked her as I put away the last remnants of the night's party.

"You bet!" However, after climbing into bed, we chattered for another hour about our families and future plans. It reminded me of the late talks I used to share with my college friends. Shortly after that, we fell asleep.

The next day we spent quietly with Vince and Ronnie until game time—which, luckily, was also their nap time. "Well, that's taken care of!" I said with relief after I settled the boys in their bedrooms. "Nap time around here is something to enjoy."

"I've gotten the station, and the game will begin in a few minutes." Jean closed the top of the stereo-radio combination.

"Good. I'll get our coffee. It's the perfect type of day to be sitting comfortably in a warm living room with a hot cup of coffee," I said, looking out our picture window at the cold, dark day.

We settled ourselves down to listen to the game. "So far, so good," remarked Jean as Marshall scored the first time. However, by the fourth quarter, it was quite evident that the game could go either way.

"This is very interesting," I said. "The player for East Carolina who's doing so much damage during this game is a boy Al used to coach in high school. Before Al left, I asked him how the boy had been doing the past few years, and he said he'd been steadily working along. I wonder what he'll have to say about him when he comes home," I chuckled.

Throughout the remainder of the game we kept hoping for a victory, but with very little time left, East Carolina scored a field goal, winning with a final score of 20-17.

"Damn!" I muttered as I sprawled out onto the couch, the height of the tension past. "It's just getting too familiar! We should have won this game, just like about three others we gave away!"

"I know what you mean," Jean said sympathetically.

"Oh well. Want some more coffee?"

"No, I'd better not. It's really getting messy outside, and I still have a lot of work to do before Gail gets home."

"I understand," I replied. "Be careful driving."

"I will. Come over for lunch next week sometime."

"Good idea," I said, walking her to the door. I noticed the steady drizzle and thought that, if the weather remained this bad, I would stay home and wait for Al, rather than go on to the airport.

CHAPTER THIRTY-FOUR

November 14, 1970

"Rubber Ducky, you're the one..." Vince and I sang together as I scrubbed him from head to toe. "How anyone can get so dirty on a rainy day is beyond me!"

"Mostly it's coloring," he said. Since he couldn't go outside in the rain, I had pacified him with a coloring book and magic markers for most of the morning and late afternoon.

"I'll tell you what," I said as he stopped pretending he was a splashing fish in the tub. "If you'll get all your toys picked up and put away, we'll sit down and watch television until Daddy comes home."

"Goody! Goody!" he shouted, clapping his wet hands together.

"Okay. Get busy, while I give Ron his bath and put him to bed," I said, smoothing down Vince's pajama top.

Al's plane was due in at about seven-thirty, and I guessed that if he came straight home, he would arrive at eight or eight-thirty. *Mission Impossible* came on, and Vince and I cuddled together on the couch to watch it. During the commercials, I jumped up and ran to the kitchen to wash or dry another dish. At about eight-twenty a picture flashed across the screen, with the word 'bulletin' written on it in large, black letters. A man's voice interrupted the programming.

"This is a special bulletin," the newsman said. "We have received word that a plane has just gone down about one-half mile from the Huntington Tri-State Airport. There is no further information at this moment."

"Mommy! Mommy! What's the matter?" I heard Vince scream, and looked down to see him pulling at my leg. I had run into the bedroom crying.

"Nothing is the matter, honey. Mommy is just being silly," I said to him as

I turned my head and wiped my eyes on the sleeve of my nightgown.

"Come on, let's go back into the living room and watch television. Mommy has to think," I said very calmly, pushing him out of the bedroom. "Just sit there and watch the end. You can tell me later if the bad man gets caught." I placed him in the big orange chair. "I'm gonna go into the kitchen and work for a little while."

I just had to think! My heart was beating hard, my hands were perspiring, and my stomach felt as if someone had just kicked it. I paced the floor wringing my hands, while moans emerged from the bottom of my throat. I sat down at the table. "Think! Think! Think!" I said aloud.

With my face in my hands and my eyes tightly closed, I went over very carefully in my mind what the man had said. There had been no indication that the plane was Al's, yet it was impossible for me to stop shaking, because I just knew it was. I looked at the wall clock. "It's eight-thirty. He isn't late getting home," I whimpered aloud, as if talking to an imaginary person would help. "God! I've got to do something! I can't just sit here!" My fist hit the top of the table.

"Mommy, when is Daddy coming home? I'm sleepy," Vince called from the living room.

"Soon...soon," I said, praying that Al would walk through the door to tease me about being such a worrier. "Mommy is going to go out for a little while, and maybe Dawn will come to play with you." Impulsively, I picked up the telephone and dialed her number, making three attempts before my fingers worked properly.

"Hello," came her voice, and I was relieved to know she was home.

"You've got to get over here right away!" I hung up before giving her time to reply, then looked up the hospital's number and dialed it.

"Hello," came the matron's answer.

"Please, you must tell me which hospital the people from the plane crash will go to," I begged.

"I'm sorry, Ma'am, but we have no information concerning the plane crash."

"Look, I've just got to know! My husband might have been on that plane, and I don't want to go out there if he might be in the hospital," I pleaded.

"I really am sorry, but there is no information, so there's no way for me to help you," she said and hung up. I called Mary Jane Tolley.

"Mary Jane, did you hear about the plane crash at the airport?" I asked immediately when she picked up the receiver.

"I heard little parts of it. Why?" she asked nonchalantly.

"I just know it's their plane," I said, trying not to sound hysterical.

"No, it couldn't be. I called earlier to find out their landing time, and someone at the airport told me that, due to inclement weather conditions, they'd probably land in Ohio."

"I'm still convinced it's their plane, and the hospital won't give out any information. If you hear anything, call me." I hung up.

I went to the door to see if any of the neighbors were home. All the houses were dark, and it seemed unbearable that no one was around to talk to. "At least someone else would tell me not to worry," I said aloud.

Dawn's car pulled into the driveway. As she came through the back door, I said, "I've just got to get out of here! I'm not sure where I'm going, and I'm so glad you're here." I knew I wasn't making too much sense, but I couldn't help it.

"Calm down, Marti. What's the matter?" she asked, lighting a cigarette.

"There's been a plane crash, and I just know it was Al's plane. I've tried to find out about it but no one knows anything. I guess I'll go over to the airport." Suddenly, my attention was caught by another news bulletin, this one on the radio.

"It has been confirmed that a DC-9 jet plane has crashed at the Huntington Tri-State Airport. However, there are no details as to which airline is involved. Stay tuned to this station and we will keep you up to date with bulletins from our reporters on the scene," the announcer said. Something in his voice told me that he knew more than he was broadcasting. It sounded very much like he'd been crying. After I heard him, I was positive that my worst fears would soon be confirmed.

I rushed out of the kitchen, leaving Vince and Ron with Dawn. As I prepared to get into the car, Doris Hanley pulled up beside me in hers.

"Wait a minute!" she shouted to me.

"I've got to hurry," I said. "I'm sure Al's plane has crashed and I've got to find out if he's all right!"

"I heard about it on the radio," she said. "That's why I'm here. I'm not going to let you drive in the state you're in. Come on, get in. I'll drive you wherever you want to go." Then I thought of Phyllis, pregnant and alone.

"Let's go to Phyllis'. I've got to make sure she's okay," I told Doris. "Stop at the drugstore first. I want to buy some cigarettes."

"I thought you quit almost a year ago," she said.

"I did," I answered. She stopped at the store and I jumped out. While waiting for the cashier to give me my change, I started crying. The gnawing sickness of not knowing was too much for me. The cashier asked no questions.

We soon arrived at Phyllis' and found the house overflowing with relatives. I had forgotten about her expected weekend visit from her parents. Deciding that I didn't want to be alone, I went inside, followed by Doris.

"Oh, Marti! Do you think it could be their plane?" Phyllis asked. I realized that enough time had passed for people to become concerned.

"I'm afraid I do," I answered her honestly. "Have they said any more about the plane?"

"They haven't announced if it was Marshall's—just that an unknown plane had crashed." I saw one of Phyllis's uncles give her some medicine and knew that she was being taken care of. The baby was due in a month, and no one wanted to see her unduly upset.

"Would you care for a drink?" someone asked me, and I refused with a shake of my head. Numbed, I sat down, not letting myself think at all. The minutes passed into nearly an hour before the radio blared again.

"We now have confirmation that the DC-9 which has crashed at the Huntington Tri-State Airport is the same DC-9 that was chartered by Marshall University to transport its football team, coaching staff and ardent fans to this afternoon's football game in North Carolina. We have no word about any survivors." The message was repeated several times, and my hopes rose at the word "survivors".

Now that it was certain Al was on board that plane, I had to call our parents to let them know before they heard it over their own television sets. I dreaded making the calls and had to force myself to the phone. Picking up the receiver, I dialed my mother's phone number. She answered almost at once.

"Mom, it's Marti," I said, choking back the tears. "I wanted to call you before you heard about it some other way. Al's plane has crashed and we're waiting to hear about the survivors."

"Oh no! Oh my God!" I heard her cry loudly from the other end. Then I heard her repeat the message to Jim, the man she would soon marry, and I was relieved to know that he was with her.

"Mom, I can't talk. I have to call the Carellis. I'll let you know something as soon as I hear." I pushed the disconnect button and dialed again, hoping it would be Dad Carelli who answered, because I didn't think I could break the news to Al's mother.

"Hello," came Dad's strong voice.

"It's Marti. Is Mom in the house?" I asked.

"She's right here. Do you want to talk to her?"

"No! I didn't want you to hear about this on television, but Al's plane has crashed. There has been no word yet about injuries," I said in a rush. It was one of the hardest things I'd ever had to say in my life.

"Oh, no!"

"I'll call you back as soon as I hear anything more. Will you be all right?" I asked him.

"Yes. We'll wait to hear from you," he said and I hung up, sick at the news I had just given them.

It was quite a while before the next radio bulletin. While I waited, I found myself reliving the nightmare of the past week when Al had been late. Then the bulletin came. No one stirred as the announcer began to speak. With my heart in my throat, I waited to find out if Al was among the lucky ones who had survived.

"Tonight at seven forty-seven," he began, "a Southern Airlines DC-9 carrying the Marshall University football team, coaching staff and some twenty townspeople crashed into the tops of some trees one-half mile short of the Huntington Tri-State Airport. The plane flipped over, hit the side of the mountain and then exploded..." He paused. "There are no survivors."

At the word "exploded", I knew that no one could have gotten out of it alive and I collapsed into Doris' open arms and cried. A tingling, empty feeling rushed through my body, and the tears didn't help to ease the pain. I knew Al was gone, that I would never see him smiling and happy again, or feel the touch of his lips or hands. He would never be a head coach or grow old. He would never see his children grow up into men, or bounce their children upon his knees. And he would never be alone as I was then.

It was over—the waiting, praying and hoping. I pulled myself together and prepared to let our parents know. Realizing that life was oftentimes hell on earth, I called the Carellis to tell them that their only son was gone.

CHAPTER THIRTY-FIVE

November 15, 1970

Doris drove me back to the house. When I entered, the kitchen was filled with mourning friends. Vincent was playing happily in the living room with Dawn. Picking him up, I carried him into his bedroom.

"You've had a really big night tonight! No more playing around—you've got to get some sleep," I told him, brushing several toy cars from his bed.

"Okay," he answered obediently and hopped into bed. I looked down at him, so snug under his covers, and wondered if he had overheard anything or if I should tell him. However, since he asked no questions, I decided that, if it were possible, I would wait until after his birthday on Monday. A party had been planned and Vince had watched with anticipation as I made the invitations. Regardless of what had just happened, I would make some effort to celebrate his birthday.

As I left his room, Dawn confronted me in the hallway. "Marti, something strange happened this evening, and I thought you'd want to know about it."

"What was that?"

"While Vince and I were sitting on the couch reading, just out of the blue he turned to me and said, 'I hear my daddy's voice.' I asked him what he had said and he repeated, 'I told you, I hear my daddy's voice.'"

"Was anyone in the house?" I asked her.

"No. It was before I even knew about what had happened."

"That makes me feel a little better, to think that somehow Al got through to him. Did he tell you what his daddy was saying to him?" I asked her.

"Because it had startled me so, I didn't think to ask him."

People remained the entire night, but I spent it wandering from room to room alone. I tried desperately to accept our loss, but Al's presence seemed so alive in all of the rooms. The dresser was still untidy from where he had dumped the contents of his pockets, unopened mail was stacked on his desk, his dirty clothes were in the hamper, and his freshly-ironed shirts were hanging on the door of the closet. Just when I thought that there were no tears left, I would begin crying again.

That night, my mind played a tug-of-war. Each time I thought I had finally faced the reality of Al's death, a car would turn into the driveway and I would run to the window to see if it was him. The nocturnal battle was not in vain, however, for by morning, I had won. The pain had not lessened, nor had the tears ceased, but I had faced reality.

That morning, instead of going to church, I went with a friend to the auditorium at Marshall. Everyone who had been involved in the disaster was asked to attend, and the auditorium was overflowing with people. As I walked to a seat, I glimpsed one of the coaches and was startled—it seemed so unusual not to see the rest of them beside him. Then I realized that he had been the coach to scout our next opponent's team, so he hadn't flown to the game.

We were told that the FBI had been called in to help with the identification of the victims, and that the process could take as long as a week. There was nothing left for us to do except wait.

Not wanting to return to the house, I had my friends, the Baylous—daughter and son-in-law of our landlords—drive me to each of the coaches' houses, so I could make sure all the other women were holding up.

The tragedy had hit everyone hard. As we drove down the four-lane highways, they were practically deserted. A stranger driving through these streets would have been able to sense that something was terribly wrong. As we went from house to house, my thoughts turned to all the children who had been left without parents, and my heart went out to them.

At that time, I still wasn't sure exactly who had been on the plane. It seemed that several switches had been made at the last minute; some who had been believed to be safe were not, and vice versa. One of these was Deke, a coach who had planned to drive back from the game, but had instead boarded the plane. Another was one of the players' fathers—unable to catch the proper flight home from North Carolina, he flew back with his son, intending to catch a plane out of Huntington.

Therefore, as I was leaving Deke's wife, I was stunned when I saw Jim Gilbert walking toward her house. When he saw me, he reached out to comfort me and I cried in his arms.

"I thought you had been on the plane," I said, looking at him in disbelief.

"I couldn't make it. My car broke down," he answered. Reaching into his pocket, he pulled out a piece of paper. "Here's the phone number of the place where I'm staying," he said, writing it down. "If you need me for anything, call. I'll be here as long as it takes." I pocketed the number and left, heading for Cokie's house—my last stop before returning home.

"Where is Cokie?" I asked the strange woman who answered the door.

"I don't believe she ought to be disturbed," she answered. I went in anyway. Not finding Cokie downstairs, I took the steps two at a time, ignoring the protests of the people in the living room. When I saw her, we embraced, sharing our grief.

"Are you going to the memorial service this evening?" she asked me.

"I didn't know there was one," I replied, "but I'd like to go."

"You okay?" she asked me, sitting down on the king-sized bed.

"Yeah, I guess so. Are you?" She nodded her head in confirmation. "I've just come from all the wives' homes and everyone is holding their own. It's Phyllis I'm concerned about," I said, pacing. I was unable to sit still.

"Has something happened to the baby?"

"No. The doctor has been called and they've been keeping her sedated. It's just that she isn't willing to accept that Frank is gone. I think her parents are taking her back with them today."

"I suppose that's best. What are you going to do?"

"I don't know, but when I finally decide, I'll be doing it as fast as I can."

"Why don't we go to the memorial service together?" she suggested.

"All right. I'll pick you up around seven," I answered and prepared to leave. "If you want someone to talk to, don't hesitate to call me."

When I arrived home, Mom and Jim, her husband-to-be, met me at the door. It was a sad, tearful reunion, and we couldn't help remembering her pleasant visit with us just a short month before.

"I know you told us all to stay put, but Jim and I flew in late this afternoon, and Danny, Rachel and Rebekah are on their way."

"It's just as well. I'm happy to see you."

"Danny was told during his birthday party and decided to leave at once. Rachel and Becky wanted to come along too, so they all began driving late last night. They should be arriving late tonight sometime," Mom said, unable to take her arm from around my shoulder. My brother and sisters and I were all close in age, and we had grown up as a tightly-knit family—it was only right that they should want to be here.

We left for the service, picking up Cokie on our way.

It was held in the gymnasium, and chairs had been placed on the gym floor for the families of the victims of the crash. It seemed like it took the entire basketball court to hold the immediate families of the seventy-five people aboard that ill-fated plane. Muffled sobs were all that could be heard.

One of the starting football players, who had previously been injured and was unable to make the trip, spoke a few words along with Father Scott, an ardent fan and adopted mascot. During the singing of the Lord's Prayer, Cokie and I clasped hands and sobbed on each other's shoulders, sharing our grief as only people who have experienced a similar situation can do. The service was a deeply emotional event, touching everyone who was present.

We drove back to the house in silence, busy with our own thoughts. Even though the house was still overflowing with people, I felt very much alone. As I scanned the rooms, I noticed that there was not one person who was unattached. Everyone had families to take care of, and I felt like I needed someone that I could talk to—someone to lean on without feeling that I was depriving him of his first responsibilities. On instinct, I took Jim Gilbert's phone number from my pocket and called him.

"Hello. Gilbert speaking."

"Jim, this is Marti. Would you mind coming over to the house?"

"I'm on my way," he answered and hung up. I felt like he was pleased to be asked to help in some way. When he arrived, I went out onto the front porch to meet him.

"Jim, just knowing that you're here is comforting," I told him, and then hesitantly asked, "Would you mind putting your arm around me? I've always had a big shoulder to cry on, and I need one now." He held me while I cried, and I was comforted.

I spent the next few hours returning calls that had arrived while I was gone. The flowers, telegrams and phone calls were coming in constantly. I had received a touching phone call from Clarence Stasavich, who had recruited Al to Lenoir Rhyne College. At that time he had been their head coach, but now, ironically, was the Athletic Director of East Carolina University and one of the last people to speak to Al before he boarded the plane. I was overwhelmed to learn of all the friends that Al had made in his short twenty-seven years.

Later that evening my brother and sisters arrived, disheveled and travel-worn. So it was that my second sleepless night was spent in the presence of those closest to Al and me.

CHAPTER THIRTY-SIX

November 16, 1970

Monday morning, Vince's birthday cake was delivered. The woman who had baked and laboriously decorated it would not accept payment. The children began arriving shortly after one o'clock for his party. Instead of the intended seven, there were more than twice that number, all bearing brightly-wrapped packages. Vince had still not been told about his father's death, but I was certain he was acutely aware that something was wrong, for he carried with him a teddy bear that he had outgrown over a year ago. Even though it was more like Christmas than a birthday party, Vince never smiled or laughed. That night, he finally asked the dreaded question.

I was sitting on the side of his bed, having just tucked him in, when he said, "Why wasn't Daddy here today?" His face was set in a deep frown, and although I had known that this moment would come, I didn't know how to answer him. Still, I had to say something.

Looking at the picture of Jesus on the bedroom wall, I said, "See the picture of Jesus over your bed?"

Vince turned to look up at it, and I continued, "Daddy is now with Him. He won't be coming home anymore because Jesus needs his help more than we do."

"But I don't want Daddy to go away. I love him," he answered, rather puzzled.

"Vincent, just because you won't be able to see Daddy any more doesn't mean that he won't see you. He'll be traveling with Jesus and will go where you go and watch over you." I didn't want to dwell on the subject of Jesus' wanting Al more than we did, because I was afraid Vince would turn his anger toward Him.

My son seemed to ponder what I had said and shortly fell asleep. Whether he had accepted my explanation, I didn't know.

Later that evening, Cokie stopped by. She had just learned that Shorty had been identified, and needed someone to talk to. She showed me his class ring that the authorities had given her, and I prayed that it wouldn't be too long before I would hear something concerning Al.

It finally happened late Tuesday afternoon. Everyone was sitting around the house waiting for the phone to ring; the morning paper had revealed that nearly half the crash victims had been identified, and that funeral services had begun for many of them.

"Mrs. Carelli, please," a male voice said as I picked up the telephone on the first ring. "Your husband has been positively identified. We have his wedding band if you would like to have it."

"Yes, please," I answered, afraid to ask about his cherished college ring.

"We'll send a man out to deliver it to the house immediately," he told me and hung up.

At last the waiting was over and plans could be made. I called the Carellis, who were arranging everything from that end, and then called the airlines to make reservations for a flight to their home on Wednesday morning.

It was a strange coincidence, but several months ago I had made reservations on that same flight for the children and myself. For Thanksgiving we had planned to fly to Al's parents' house, where he would have met us after traveling a recruiting circuit. I had mixed up the dates and made the reservations for a week too soon, only canceling them Saturday, the day of the game. Now, as fate would have it, we were rescheduling the same reservations for the same day and time.

Thirty minutes later, there was a knock on the door. Unable to get up to answer it, I was still sitting at the kitchen table when Jim spoke to me from the living room.

"Marti, it's the ring."

"I don't want to take it unless you can read the date inscribed on the inside," I said, my voice rising.

"It says 'MEB to ACC 6-6-66'," Jim read softly.

"All right, bring it here," I said dully. When he put the blackened gold ring into my hand, I realized the finality of Al's death. Whatever small hope that might have remained within my subconscious mind was gone when my fingers encircled the wedding band that Al hadn't removed from his finger since the day we were married. Suddenly, I needed to get away from the house and asked Jim to take me for a drive.

On the drive, I tried to explain to Jim that I knew Al was safe and happy, and that we mourned for ourselves because of his absence. We had been left behind to continue patiently with life's daily struggles, until the time when we could be reunited with each other and God. The extremely one-sided conversation helped me to relax. When Jim returned me to my home, I was able to sleep for the first time since Al's death.

The following day, the troupe of relatives gathered at my house flew together to the Carellis' to attend the viewing and funeral.

I had brought two pictures of Al with me. One had been taken when he was a senior in college, and the other when he was coaching at Marshall. These I put into the frame that was to be placed on top of the coffin for the night of the viewing.

When I arrived at the funeral home, I tried not to enter the room where the coffin was, because I wanted to remember Al's living presence and not this silent one. But at the urging of Mom Carelli, I at last ventured into the largest of the three rooms.

I was startled at the sight of hundreds of flower arrangements, which filled each room. While I waited for the arrival of our friends, I walked from bouquet to bouquet, reading the messages sent from every person we had known, realizing how many lives Al had touched. When I saw the flowers from the family covering the coffin, I wept. The sparkling, glittering words, "Dear Daddy" stood out, and I thought of our two sons who still did not understand the depth of what had happened.

Many people came that night to pay their respects to Al, and I was stunned at the multitude of people who had driven great distances to be present. I was saddened that Al wasn't able to greet them too, for he would have been so happy to have walked and talked with them.

We left late that evening, knowing that the next day would bring the final farewell...the funeral.

In the morning, I woke to the brightness of the sun shining through my bedroom window, and felt it unfair that the day should be so beautiful. We arrived at the church and greeted the nine pallbearers who were some of Al's closest friends—college roommates, high school friends, and acquaintances made through coaching. John Dupree had flown in the night before from New Mexico, Becky and Tony McClamrock, along with Gene Abercrombie, had driven in from North Carolina.

"Are you ready, Mrs. Carelli?" the funeral director asked me when the coffin and bearers were in position to enter the church.

"Yes," I answered, and he showed me where to stand in the procession. It was cold, and I was relieved that I had decided on wearing my black knee-high vinyl boots instead of heels. I also wore the red dress that Al had loved so much, with my black vinyl raincoat over it to please the traditionally-minded people.

As we walked down the aisle of the church, I spotted my oldest friend and her husband, Lana and Bob France, sitting in a side pew. In a flash, I remembered their visit to Huntington for one of our home games. It had been raining, and Lana had gone with me to pick up the boots that I was now wearing.

Bringing my attention back to the service, I listened. As the words "ashes to ashes" were spoken, I thought how people tend to forget—or strive to push the thought from their minds—that death is inevitable. I also realized that, if death should strike near me again, the pain of it would not lessen for my having experienced it before.

The ride to the cemetery seemed to take hours instead of minutes. As we pulled into our reserved parking place, I looked behind me to see the cars lined up the entire length of the highway.

The service from that point on was short, and with the closing prayer, it was over. The funeral director handed me a white flower, and told me I should put it on top of the coffin before I left the gravesite, as a last tribute. I felt one flower would be incomplete, so I asked the director to hand me two small roses. As I placed one on either side of my white flower, I said, "This one is for Vincent, and this one is for Ronald!"

I spoke loudly, for in that instant, I was angry that God had seen fit to take Al before his sons had learned to know him. Yet as soon as the words were spoken, I knew that it would be impossible for them not to know him. He had taught me so much, and I in turn would teach them what I had learned. I believed that for some reason unknown to me, our boys had been left for me to raise, and I did not want to disappoint Al. I spoke my final farewell within the silence of my mind, turned, and retraced my steps to the black limousine which would take me to our boys and the new life we were forced to begin.

EPILOGUE

March 25, 1973

I replaced the gray typewriter into its black case. The story that I had set out to write nearly two years ago was finally completed. It hadn't been too difficult to compose, but there had been little time, peace or quiet in which to work.

I walked upstairs to the children's bedrooms and noticed that one of the bunk beds was empty. Straining to hear footsteps on the carpet, I surprised Vince as he came out of the bathroom.

"Vincent, what are you doing out of bed?" I asked him sternly, since it was nearly eleven o'clock.

"I was thirsty, so I got myself a drink," he said in his own defense. I looked at him and saw the spitting image of his father.

"You may be all of five and a half years old, but that doesn't entitle you to go traipsing around the house at all hours of the night," I scolded, watching until he had safely climbed the ladder to the top bunk.

"Goodnight, Mom. I love you." He certainly was a lovable fellow, and my sternness dissolved into the air.

"Goodnight, love," I said and stretched my arms over the top of the guardrail to give him a hug. Then, stooping beneath the upper bunk, I paused long enough to replace Ronnie's fallen pillow under his blond head. At nearly three, he was as stubborn as a mule and needed much discipline and affection. I bent down and kissed his peaceful face.

Turning, I crossed the hall into Kelly and Andy's room. As I caressed Kelly's long blonde hair and pulled the slipping cover over Andy's shoulder, a thought struck me. Retracing my steps down the stairs, I pulled my typewriter out of its case once more and began to type.

March 25, 1973

My Dearest Kelly,

Tonight I've finished my story, written for your brothers, Vince and Ronnie. However, I feel that it would be incomplete if I didn't express how wonderfully happy I am that you are now a part of the family.

Kelly, six months after your Uncle Al was killed, you came to us lost and confused. Your mother, my youngest sister, had just separated from your father, and was not financially able to take care of you. Because she loved you so much, she allowed me to care for you in the way that she couldn't. She worked hard in the hope that, one day, you could be reunited.

However, the longer you stayed with us, the more attached we became to you, and you to us. Vince and Ronnie were like your older and younger brothers. To me, you became the daughter I never had.

Your mother, seeing how happy and well-adjusted you had become, put aside her own personal feelings in favor of yours.

So it was that, after living with us for nearly two years, you were adopted. We had become five instead of four.

This June you will be five years old, a darling daughter to cherish, and I am very proud of you.

Love,
Mother

I stood up and stretched my cramped body. Lighting a cigarette, a habit I had never been able to lick again, I went to the stove and poured myself another cup of coffee. Besides Kelly there was now Andy, so returning to the kitchen table, I began again.

March 25, 1973

My Dearest Andy,

*   You have made us six instead of five, and the joy you have brought to us all cannot be expressed in mere words. You are fortunate in having Vince as your protector, Kelly as your little mother, and Ronnie as your overly rough playmate. Together they share in the happiness that emanates from you, their own baby brother.*

*   Over the years we have struggled to get where we are, and with your birth five months ago, we have attained it: we have become a complete, unique family.*

*   You are my last-born, and I hope for you, as I do for all of my children, that someday you will be blessed with a beautiful family as I have been.*

Love,
Mother

My thoughts turned to Jim and the part he had played in our lives. For months after the crash, he had always been around whenever help was needed. That first Christmas had been full of excitement because he put up the tree and brought the presents. No matter where in the world we traveled, if there was ever an obstacle, Jim had been as close as the telephone. He had taught Vince to speak up when children made unkind remarks about him for having no living father. And when spring arrived, it was inevitable that we would begin seeing each other in a new light. It was in September that we were married, and my children welcomed their second daddy eagerly.

With these thoughts in mind, I composed my letter to Jim.

March 25, 1973

My Dearest Jim,

*   What can I say but that, without you, we would be nothing. I know of only one way to tell our story—so I have written this poem.*

KISMET CONSUMMATED

In anguish you came to us that sorrow-filled Sunday,
Wandering amidst the excruciating pain that constantly stabbed us to our
   very souls,
Only to leave in its destructive wake the realization
That death is the end of life on Earth and man finds
Comfort in the living presence of one another.

A sympathetic glance—an encouraging word—understanding;
Children—time for attention and play—distraction;
A comforting embrace—tears gently brushed away—compassion;
A ring, a wedding ring—pressed firmly into the hand of another—spiritual
   comfort.

Laughter, confusion, decorations strewn upon the floor;
Excited children watch in awe within the comfort of their home,
While icy winds wistfully rap upon windowpanes,
Catching a glimpse of a Christmas tree surrounded by presents,
   children and you—a friend true.

Melting snows, soft earth—Winter vanishes;
Sunshine, serenity—Spring arrives in all its glory;
Your hand in mine—hope is renewed as we gaze at the heavens above;
Within the black velvety softness of the clouds, a lone star appears.

Its radiance envelopes us—its warmth fills our souls;
Shed of its horror, the past is revealed—a pleasant memory to be cherished;
Beneath the star's twinkling radiance we embrace—cling one to another;
Together we strive for happiness, security, love, reality—life.

Love,
Marti

As I finished, I felt the weight of time lift from my shoulders. I walked into our living room as inner peace and happiness engulfed my entire being. I gazed up at the large gilded portrait of our four children and knew that the past could never be changed, and the future was still to be molded.

REFLECTIONS 1990

January, 1990

Twenty years! As the small black sports car wound its way up the steep gravel drive, the crunching of tires on gravel pierced the quiet of the early morning. Except for a scattering of evergreens, the trees were bare. The sky was a murky gray, casting an eerie glow over the tombstones in Springhill Cemetery. The car came to a halt and the door opened. I stepped out into the bitter cold.

The wind whipped about my bare head, tousling my short brown hair and forcing me to pull the collar of my blue winter jacket protectively about my neck. I shoved my gloveless hands deep into my pockets searching for warmth, and shivered. Twenty years!

****

For a while I had toyed with the idea of republishing *Kismet Consummated: A Mother's Memoir*, my book about my life with Al. Tucked away in the back of my filing cabinet was a folder containing letters received over the years with requests for copies of the original book. Some of the requests came from people who never had the opportunity to read the book, while others had simply lost their original copy and wanted a replacement.

It was often difficult for me to understand what people derived from reading the book, since I had only written it and had never read it in its entirety. Yet over the years, the positive feedback encouraged me to believe that it had some worth, and that republishing was a valid course of action.

To be quite honest, there was a secondary reason for republishing. Although writing *Kismet* was a draining experience, it made me realize that I had a true passion for writing. This passion I have been able to realize with the completion of my second book and through actively working on my third, both novels. Republishing my first book would complete a circle of sorts.

Once the decision was made to republish, I felt an obligation to the reader to fill in the gap of the last twenty years. A second part of the book was out of the question, so it was that I decided to simply add a section entitled *Reflections*.

****

Hesitantly, I walked from the car to the edge of the well-kept, grassy area. From this knoll high above the city of Huntington, the Marshall University towers were visible in the distance. The wind whipped against my face, forcing me to hunch my shoulders in an effort to trap the warmth within my coat. I began to shiver, but wasn't sure if it was entirely from the cold.

I glanced back at the grassy knoll, glimpsing the six grave markers nestled within the ice-covered grass. Beyond them towered a large stone monument with two pathways leading to its central point. Thirty-two boxwoods bordered the area, and two stone benches offered a convenient resting place for visitors. There were several bouquets of flowers placed around the area, the cards still attached, addressed to a loving member of some family whose name appeared somewhere on the stone monument.

Tears filled my eyes as I read, "They shall live in the hearts of their families and friends forever and this memorial records their loss to the university and to the community." This was addressed to all those whose names appeared on the monument, including the six boys whose graves were beneath my feet.

Each side of the monument listed different names. The second side listed staff members—twelve; and airline crew members—five; the third side listed alumni and friends—twenty-one, including eight couples; and the fourth side listed the members of the football team—thirty-seven. I returned to the second side, pulled my hand from my pocket and ran my fingers across the cold stone where the name "Albert Carl Carelli, Jr." was etched. Above, I read, "In lasting remembrance of the Marshall University football team, the coaches, staff and devoted fans who died in the plane crash November 14, 1970."

I had returned. The trip from Nashville, Tennessee to Huntington, West Virginia was well thought out. I came with the full intention of reliving my experiences.

Life is sometimes so very strange. A word, a song, a look, an incident can trigger the mind so that time has no meaning and a span of twenty years is diminished in a mere second. As I brushed my fingers over Al's name, the hurt returned, and the grief that had been buried for so many years burst forth, carrying with it the same pain of loss and fear of the unknown that I had felt in 1970.

The cold won. Its biting edge penetrated to my soul, forcing me to turn from this place in search of a warmer location. As I restarted the car I realized a certain weight had been lifted from my shoulders. And yet, as the car wound its way down the narrow road, I knew it was merely the first step.

****

Jim was almost twenty-six years old when our fourth child was born. Together we raised Vincent, Kelly, Ronald and Andrew. Together we instilled in them a belief in God and taught them the values of love, honesty, sincerity, hard work, self-worth and confidence. Together we guided them through childhood, adolescence and into young adulthood. We truly gave them roots and wings. There is a wonderful bond of love and mutual respect between the children and Jim. The children themselves are a true testament to the love and care they received from their father. I am both pleased and proud of him.

It was a tragedy that brought us together, and our unwillingness to change that separated us. After eighteen years of marriage Jim and I have decided to go our separate ways. We remain friends, secure in the knowledge that we have been good for one another, yet recognizing that the direction of our lives no longer runs along the same path. There is a time for everything.

****

Quietly, I pushed my chair away from the oak-topped table in the small, warm restaurant where I had stopped to write. I yawned, stretched. I had been writing for several hours and was beginning to feel the emotional drain. The sun had come up, giving the false impression that beyond the giant picture window it was a warm, clear day. The mutterings of the customers as they paraded through the large wooden doors proved that appearances can be deceiving—the temperature still remained in the low teens.

"More coffee?" the trim young waitress questioned as I shifted into a more comfortable position.

"Always," I answered with a nod of my head. Fortunately, the place was not too busy, for I was not quite ready to leave. I wondered if the waitress realized that I was literally renting her table. I looked at my watch and saw that the time was slipping by rapidly. Picking up my pen, I continued to write.

****

Andrew, at seventeen, is a natural-born athlete who is plagued by all the normal crises that confront teenagers today. He is struggling with his belief in God, desperately trying to understand females, and searching for his own niche within a family of proven athletes. As a junior in high school, he is committed to college athletics, either in football or baseball.

As a youngster, he was extremely close to his sister Kelly, and misses her tremendously. Vincent was always the one he looked up to, and it wasn't until

Vince left for college that Andy was able to establish a closer relationship with Ronald. Yet recently, being thrown together for several years has forged a bond between them that seems to be growing stronger with each passing day. Andrew is the sensitive one, the one who is in the middle of his search.

****

One more stretch, one more cup of black coffee, one more notation before returning to Don and Carolyn Baylous' home in Barboursville. Ever since our first meeting twenty years ago, they have remained steadfast friends who always welcomed me or Jim at a moment's notice—no matter the time, the day or the year. Once again I was there for "Bed and Breakfast."

****

Picking up my pen, I turned my thoughts to Kelly, my adopted daughter. Hers is a face that could have launched a thousand ships. Her eyes are hazel and almond-shaped. Her hair, nose, mouth and cheekbones are every woman's dream. As a child, she was adorable; as a woman, beautiful.

She came to us when she was nearly three and left when she was nineteen. Over the years it was often difficult for her to adjust to having two families—one in California, one in Tennessee. Both families thought of her as an integral part of their lives and successfully kept a good balance for her. After her second year in college, she moved to California permanently to live with her other family. In November of 1989, she married David Rochow and presently lives in California. The boys miss her. We all miss her. One chapter closes only for another to begin, and life goes on for our dearest Kelly.

****

Early the morning after my arrival in Huntington, the chimes from the alarm located next to the bed rang quietly. It was a sound I could live with. The tiny alarm clock, a gift from my mother, was a treasure. Not until I began using it did I fully realize that the shrill alarm of earlier days had adversely affected my attitude for several hours each morning. It was as startling a discovery to me as learning, years ago in college, that I was able to memorize information written in green ink much more quickly than information written in blue ink.

Eagerly I jumped out of bed, quickly showered and dressed. With a cup of hot coffee in hand, I walked from the warmth of the house into the icy darkness outside. The only sound was the crunching of my footsteps upon the frozen grass. It seemed so odd that at seven a.m. it was pitch black.

The car started easily. While I waited for it to warm up, I thought about what was next. I had allowed myself several days to complete *Reflections*, and I was now at the midpoint. I decided to return to the restaurant I'd stopped at the day before. There I could find coffee and just the right amount of noise to aid in my concentration.

When writing, I am most comfortable away from home situations. My dream, however, is to build a log home on an eighty-acre tract of land I own on the outskirts of Nashville. From there, in the midst of that near-wilderness, my imagination can soar. The sounds of nature, the scurrying noises of the various animals, all welcome me. It is there that I find peace.

When I arrived at the restaurant, it was empty and quiet. I began again.

****

It is very painful for me to think back on one particular period in my son Ronald's life. Perhaps it is because I feel responsible—as an educator, I should have recognized that he was having more than the average difficulty in school. Inconceivably, an entire bitter and frustrating year passed before he was helped.

When Ronald was in fourth grade, it was obvious that he was having a hard time learning. What was not obvious was that he was being tormented and abused by several teachers. He later gave me many examples of this, but the one that stands out in my mind involved a spat between Ronald and a younger boy. As punishment, the teacher, assuming it was Ronald's fault since he was the oldest, allowed the younger boy to paddle him. During an assembly, he singled out Ronald and related the occurrence to the entire school. The humiliation was compounded by the fact that his younger brother, Andrew, was present in the audience.

The incident that truly brought home the seriousness of Ronald's situation occurred one morning before he was to leave for school. I heard a strange muffled noise coming from his room. When I approached, I realized that he was sobbing in his closet. I opened the door to find his small form huddled in a darkened corner. His sobbing was devastating, a sound I will never forget.

Between his choked sobs, he cried, "I wish I was dead!"

When I heard that statement, I was sick, frightened, confused. For anyone to mutter those words would have been serious. For a child of ten, it was shocking.

Fortunately, it was a turning point. Immediately we had him tested by professionals and were informed that he had a learning disability. We enrolled Ronald in a special school for the next four years. By ninth grade, he was able to attend Father Ryan High School, and later successfully graduated. He has excelled as a catcher in baseball and is presently a red-shirted freshman on an athletic scholarship at Cleveland State Community College in Cleveland, Tennessee.

Today, Ron looks very much like Al. A loving, caring person, he dares to be different and dreams of playing professional baseball.

****

My mind and my hand were tired. The waitress was truly humoring me this time; my coffee cup was never empty. Soon, however, I noticed the place was beginning to get crowded, and knew my table was needed. I had two more stops to make, so I carefully packed everything into my leather briefcase, said goodbye to my patient waitress and returned to the car. I headed toward the university.

Over the past twenty years, many changes had been made on campus. One of the most impressive was the new Memorial Student Center. A memorial fountain had been built on the plaza and inside, to the right of the main entrance, were placed a picture of the team and a plaque dedicating the Center to the memory of those who lost their lives November 14, 1970.

Ironically, the majority of the students attending the university now had not even been born at that time. It was not to this area that I was going.

At last, after many wrong turns, I found the narrow road cramped between the old athletic building and Hodges Hall. Behind the athletic building was the empty practice field, my destination. I parked the car and ran across the uneven brick street, noticing that the buildings were old and in disrepair. A chain link fence bordered the sidewalk. I leaned into the fence, my fingers curling around its worn thick wires. As I gazed at the field, I could see the players, hear the coaches shouting out commands, smell the sweat that glistened on their faces, dripped from their hair and soaked their shirts. I could even visualize young Vincent beside me, tugging at my leg, begging to be lifted higher so he could watch the activity from a better perspective.

All ghosts—ghosts disappearing into the mist. I shook my head to clear it, and walked around the fence to the spot where I had visualized the team just seconds ago. I bent down and touched the earth. It was the same earth, a different time. I stood up. Once more it was quiet. I was alone.

I walked to the side of the field where a pit had been built, perhaps for track events. Weeds and grass had taken it over. Certainly it held its own stories. However, for now, I sat on the edge of it, ignoring the cold and thinking back to another time, to another similar field when Vincent was only six years old.

****

He was sitting on the players' bench on the home side of the football field. Intently, he watched the flag football game. Whenever something favorable occurred, he stood up and cheered his team. Whenever there was a setback, he would hop up, stomp his foot and run his small fingers through his unruly dark hair. Often he glanced at his coach in anticipation.

Soon the game ended—the team had won, but Vince hadn't played. It was his very first game; the disappointment was etched on his face. Kneeling down so that he and Vince were on the same level, Jim said, "Cheer up, Vince. You won!"

"But, Dad," he replied, "I didn't help. I didn't get to play." The tears spilled over onto his cheeks. Jim held him close.

"You did help. You practiced with this team every day. Without you, they wouldn't have known how to play to win." He wiped away Vince's tears. "Come on, Vince. It's only the beginning. Your time will come," Jim stated, taking the small hand in his big one. Together they left the park.

It was only the beginning. For the next few years, Vince played football in an organized youth program. From the start, he was a quarterback. I always thought it began that way because he was able to remember the plays without the coaches having to write them on his hand!

In seventh grade, he earned the starting quarterback position. In eighth grade, he lost it due to a separated growth line in his right shoulder. Unable to throw a ball for an entire year, he played tight end.

In ninth grade, Vince attended Father Ryan High School, where it was a never-ending battle for the quarterback slot. For the end of his junior year and the beginning of his senior year he started at that position. When the coaches moved him to tight end in the middle of his senior year, his hopes for an athletic scholarship were dashed. Even so, his dream lived on.

After Vince spent one football season at TMI (formerly Tennessee Military Institute), several colleges showed an interest in him, including Marshall University. By January of 1987 he made the decision to walk on at the University of Tennessee in Chattanooga, a Southern Conference School. By the 1987 football season, Vince had earned a scholarship and was red-shirted.

In 1988, as an eligible freshman player, he earned a starting position for the last three games of the season. The 1989 season opened with him at the starting slot, and he led UTC to a 14-0 victory over Marshall University in 1989. For the remainder of the season, however, UTC was plagued with several close losses and Vincent was benched after the sixth game. He saw no real action again until the fourth quarter of the last game.

****

My legs were beginning to cramp from sitting cross-legged. I stood up, stretched, and took a look around. This time I saw students scurrying from one building to another, some struggling with large musical instruments. I walked back to the car, started its engine and turned from the side street into the busy traffic. I was very near the end of my journey. There was only one more stop.

True, I had been there last year for the game between UTC and Marshall. I was also there ten years before for the memorial weekend, and once when Jim played in an alumni game. But now I needed to see the playing field this way—deserted.

Slowly, I approached, noticing that the field took up an entire city block. Today, the gates were chained and sheets of Astroturf had been carelessly piled to one side. It had been twenty years since I had seen that football field empty.

I parked the car in an illegal zone and walked to one of the locked gates. Briefly, I considered climbing the fence, only to dismiss the idea as too visible. I looked around, but experienced no sadness, no "feel" for that last game. Instead, my thoughts raced ahead to the game to be played October 20, 1990, between Marshall and UTC. It would be the last game UTC ever played on this field, since Marshall's new field was to be completed by the 1991 season.

The idea was uncanny! Vincent, who had celebrated his third birthday just two days after his father's death, would return to play on this field on nearly the same date of the last game that his father coached twenty years before! It was history in the making.

What an experience, this return trip! I left the field in good spirits. As I drove back to Barboursville, I reflected on what was next for Vince. Actually, quite a lot—including two more years of eligibility.

Driving through the sunny hills, my heart was light and my burdens diminished. I smiled as I remembered the poem that I had asked Vince to memorize that eighth-grade year when he momentarily thought he might never be a quarterback again.

"Come on, Vince, just one more time," I whispered to myself. Then magically, he was thirteen and the mellow sounds of his young voice filled my ear.

> *"If you think you are beaten, you are,*
> *If you think you dare not, you don't.*
> *Success begins with your own will...*
> *It's all in your state of mind.*
>
> *"Life's battles are not always won*
> *By those who are stronger or faster;*
> *Sooner or later the person who wins*
> *Is the person who thinks he can!"*

Often, people have referred to me as courageous. It was an idea that I rejected. Then, one day I came across the following line: "Courage is simply the willingness to be afraid and to act anyway." What a revelation! Are we not all courageous every day of our lives?